Good Morning, Mr. Paul

A Memoir of a Peace Corps
Volunteer's Journey into History

Paul Burghdorf

WestBow
PRESS
A DIVISION OF THOMAS NELSON

WestBow Press books may be ordered through booksellers or by contacting:

WestBow Press
A Division of Thomas Nelson
1663 Liberty Drive
Bloomington, IN 47403
www.westbowpress.com
1-(866) 928-1240

ISBN: 978-1-4497-7091-4 (e)
ISBN: 978-1-4497-7092-1 (sc)
ISBN: 978-1-4497-7093-8 (hc)

Library of Congress Control Number: 2012918969

Printed in the United States of America

WestBow Press rev. date: 11/01/2012

Contents

May 20th, 2015

To David,

May you always seek purpose and adventure in your life.

Carpe Diem,
Paul Burghdof
Cabin 268

Acknowledgments

In writing *Good Morning, Mr. Paul,* I have had the joy of interacting with many friends, neighbors, colleagues, and family who have cheered me on. Without a doubt, I am indebted to my faithful wife, Marilyn, for her editing skills and persistent encouragement. Together, we have enjoyed recalling memories and sharing our love for Indonesia. Thanks go to my grandchildren, children, and their spouses—Kristin, Andrew, and Jen; Kim and Ken Shemwell; Sage and Isabelle—for standing by me. They endured reading and rereading written chapters, even though they know these stories by heart from childhood.

The cheering squad has included friends from near and far, too many to list, but there are a few that I must include. Ross Miller, you gifted me with a listening ear, a joyous spirit, and honest feedback. The Montrose Barbershop provided an interesting book critiquing forum. Ron and Jack met with me over coffee early Saturday mornings to provide feedback to my Indonesian adventures before Jack placed copies alongside the newspapers in his barbershop. Additionally, I feel privileged to have interacted with the many unnamed neighbors and friends who certainly are not forgotten. Thank you.

From my years with the Peace Corps, I have renewed contacts, a blessing I had not anticipated. When I contacted Alex Shakow, my in-country director during my years in Indonesia, he offered to share the extensive files that he had kept on me during those memorable years. What valuable, insightful reading those papers have provided me! Contacts with Jim Noonan and Dick Doughty provided rewarding conversations, and their responses to chapters involving them certainly kept my accounts accurate. *Terima kasih,* my friends.

WestBow Press is represented well by Maggie England, my publishing consultant. She has been vital in helping me transform my experiences from my head and heart to the printed page.

Cheers to my awesome cheering team.

Preface

I arrived in Palembang, South Sumatra, in the 1960s as a shy, idealistic young man who aspired to tackle President John F. Kennedy's challenge, "Ask not what your country can do for you, but ask what you can do for your country," by serving as a Peace Corps volunteer coaching Indonesian athletes for the 1964 Olympic Games in Japan. Little did I realize, however, that my myopic view of the world would drastically change in the crucible experiences and the etching events that shaped my life from 1963–1965. My two "years of living dangerously" in some ways paralleled the harrowing events portrayed in the movie *The Year of Living Dangerously*. My experiences would alter my value system, strengthen my faith, and change the course of my life forever.

Good Morning, Mr. Paul chronicles my experiences through vignettes—some hilarious and some not so funny—depicting my relationships, work, and daily life in Indonesia. It is, perhaps more significantly, about a young man with a limited worldview learning that people are far more important than things; that the measure of a man, even an athlete, lies not in his physical strength but in his courage to continue when there seems little hope; that it is better to serve others than to be served; that faith is real.

In so many ways, I received more from my Peace Corps service than I gave. As readers follow my adventures in Indonesia, I trust the memoir will challenge fellow travelers of all ages to service by reaching out to others and by sharing in our common humanity despite our wonderful differences. Such life priorities position one on paths with amazing twists and often divine surprises. While the book speaks to all ages, it is my hope that my fellow baby boomers, now facing retirement, will hear President Kennedy's call, not to ask what will be given to them but what they can still give, perhaps by "retiring for *good*."

1
Good Morning, Mr. Paul

Night had long laid its blanket of darkness upon Palembang, South Sumatra, by the time I had finished a *Hamlet* tutorial for future English teachers who were studying at the University of Sriwidjaja. With the *Hamlet* tutorial over, students were saying their goodbyes and slowly departing from Wang's Tea House. I picked up my lecture notes and started across General Sudirman Boulevard, the main street of Palembang. Suddenly I heard a youthful, strident voice yelling, "Good morning, Mr. Paul! Good morning!" I quickly glanced in the direction of this blustering greeting to see a dilapidated, black bike menacingly heading in my direction. For several long seconds, the rider and I waltzed together, with me precariously straddled across the front fender of the bike like a hood ornament on an old Chrysler. With impending doom, I screamed, *"Berhenti! Berhenti!"* (Stop! Stop!) Out of the urge for self-preservation, I lunged for the safety of the far curb. As I picked myself up, along with my scattered lecture notes, I surfaced to face Omar from my morning English as a Second Language class. That very morning we had been practicing simple phrases such as *good morning* and *good evening*—evidently not well enough. I shouted back at Omar, "It's 'good evening,' not 'good morning!'" Even with that quick English lesson review, Omar rode off with great confidence, incorrectly replying, "Good morning, Mr. Paul. Good morning!"

Feeling frustrated and somewhat deflated as an English teacher, I started my slow trek home. Since it was late at night and darkness had masked the sky, I opened the door to those questions of self-doubt, perhaps similar ones that gnaw at most humans. "What am I doing here

1

in Indonesia? What makes me think I can teach, especially English as a second language?" Perhaps the most introspective of all: "How did a California boy like me end up in this crazy, topsy-turvy, upside-down world of Indonesia?"

With these disturbing questions on my mind, I drifted back three years to 1960 and to John F. Kennedy's inaugural address. One might even say it was President Kennedy's fault; yeah, it was *his* fault! Kennedy's memorable lines, "Ask not what your country can do for you; ask what you can do for your country," were revolutionary for many people, including this Southern California college graduate. Kennedy's appeal for service to my country and to mankind caught my imagination; in fact, it set my passion for service aflame.

Kennedy's challenge still burned within me two years later during the dog days of summer in Southern California. I had just completed my degree in English and my secondary teaching credential at Pasadena College. My years of study there had been formative. In fact, my love of literature and many of my life perspectives stem from my years at Pasadena College and from the influence of dedicated professors there.

While I was awaiting the start of my teaching career at Pasadena Academy, I continued to reflect on what I wanted to do with my life. As I was leaving my apartment one afternoon, a friend asked me if I wanted to see *Breakfast at Tiffany's.* Feeling the boredom of summer and wanting companionship on a Friday afternoon, I decided to join her. The film, a romance comedy, would soon be forgotten, but the theme song was catchy and haunting. Phrases such as "two drifters off to see the world" and "there is such a lot of world to see" caused me to reflect back on Kennedy's words. Suddenly, I realized that I wanted to widen my perspective of the world and to expand my horizons. Yes, I would be a "drifter off to see the world," but a drifter with a purpose! Now I had my marching orders. "Ask not what your country can do for you; ask what you can do for your country" was no longer just Kennedy's motto. It was mine, also! The next day, I posted my letter requesting a Peace Corps application.

2
Making Hard Choices

Burghdorf, why would you join the Peace Corps? Where will you go? You have everything going for you here. What about finishing graduate school? Why would you leave your girlfriend and your university buddies to join a government program that very few people know or even care about? Are you sure that you will be paid only three dollars in-country each month, with a clothing allowance of one hundred dollars yearly? Big deal that you will receive fifteen hundred in severance pay. Is this the reality of President John F. Kennedy's glorious vision? How could he mean what he said: "Life in the Peace Corps will not be easy. There will be no salary, and allowances will be at a level sufficient only to maintain health and meet basic needs. Men and women will be expected to work and live alongside the nationals of the country in which they are stationed—doing the same work, eating the same food, talking the same language"? Question after question came from family members and friends.

Similar questions had dominated my thinking ever since I had filled out that voluminous application several months prior. Why would I give up a good job teaching English at Pasadena Academy and working as the athletic director? Why would I put my M.A. and teaching credential on hold for several years? Did I really want to embark on a vague future?

As a teacher, I also knew that I had to live up to the challenge I had given my high school students. "Make the hard choices, difficult choices that stretch one mentally, physically, and spiritually. Those choices are what build strength of character." Truly, such advice is easier said than done. Rather than demonstrating by our own life choices, we educators

3

and leaders so often resort simply to telling young people to make the more difficult choices. Where are the inspiring role models for our young people? Where are those who put actions to their words?

"Burghdorf, what's holding you back? Get going!" I concluded.

Months later, the telegram from Washington, D.C., read:

I am pleased to inform you that you have been selected to participate in a Peace Corps training program for Indonesia. Training begins mid February. Details to follow by letter. Congratulations.

Robert Sargent Shriver Jr.,
Director Peace Corps

Even today, fifty years later, as I pen my memoir, I recall the excitement I felt being one of nineteen coaches selected out of 250 applicants to train Indonesians for the 1964 Olympic Games in Japan. Although young and inexperienced, I had chosen the challenging "road not taken," which would definitely make all the difference in my life, as I now look back on that decision.

I had indicated on my Peace Corps application that West Africa was my area of preference, but Indonesia was to be my assignment. Frankly, like Christopher Columbus, I did not have a clue where Indonesia was located geographically. In school, I had heard of the Dutch East Indies, not Indonesia. Without a doubt, this was ignorance on my part that time and travel would rectify. My initial research revealed that Indonesia is the fifth largest country in the world in terms of population. Java is the most densely populated place on earth per square mile. Indonesia is the world's largest archipelago, which consists of 17,200 islands (depending on the tide) and that spans a distance of over three thousand miles and three time zones. Of the 17,200 islands, only six thousand are populated. The more famous islands are Java, Sumatra, Kalimantan, Bali, and New Guinea.

After World War II, Indonesia fought against the Dutch for its independence, which they received in 1948. Indonesia became a "guided democracy" under President Sukarno in 1957. "Guided" equated to Bung Sukarno balancing and maintaining his political control by pitting his army, the largest standing army in Southeast Asia, against Indonesia's communist party (PKI), the largest communist party outside of any communist country at that time. This was at a time in history when competition and fears between capitalism and communism motivated

4

world politics. The Berlin Wall was real! The issue of dominance in science spurred reforms in American education and space exploration, commonly referred to as the "space race." Many people still remember the television footage of Nikita Khrushchev, the leader of the Soviet Union, pounding the podium as he challenged and threatened the free world with: "We will bury you!" China was the "sleeping giant," and Viet Nam had erupted. The West, fearing the "domino effect" in Southeast Asia, debated where to draw the line against the expansion of Chinese communism in the area. Southwest of Viet Nam lay resource-rich Indonesia, where Sukarno also encouraged confrontation between the Old Established Forces (the Western influence of the United States, Britain, and Holland) and the New Emerging forces (Viet Nam, Cambodia, Thailand, Malaysia, and Indonesia).

Initially, my knowledge of Indonesia originated from statistics and facts but did not encompass the rich culture or gracious spirit of the Indonesian people. With Indonesia's independence, the law required all Indonesians to officially record their religious preference. Statistics reveal that Islam is the dominant religion in Indonesia, accounting for approximately 90 percent of the people. The other 10 percent is composed primarily of Christians, Hindus, and animists. Only by living and working side by side with the Indonesians, however, would I eventually come to realize the significant "facts" about the country and people, realities that have endeared Indonesia to me for more than fifty years.

Experiences that I would weave into my limited perspective of the truth of President Kennedy's words awaited me. Those words were, at that time, only romantic and idealistic phrases to me: "But if the life will not be easy, it will be rich and satisfying. For every young American who participates in the Peace Corps—who works in a foreign land—will know that he or she is sharing in the great common task of bringing to man that decent way of life that is the foundation of freedom and a condition of peace."

With my limited knowledge of Indonesia, I entered Peace Corps training at Iowa University on February 22, 1963, in the frozen cold of winter. I still cannot understand why Iowa University was selected rather than Hilo, Hawaii, the regular site for the Far East area programs. Even though the geography and the weather did not lend themselves in training coaches for Indonesia, the University of Iowa did have excellent programs in sports training and English studies. And to be fair, our assignment was to train Indonesian athletes for the 1964 Olympic Games in Japan.

Nineteen candidates arrived in Iowa City on that cold February 22, 1963, to begin an adventure that would affect our lives forever.

I anxiously sat in the front seat next to the window of an Ozark DC-3, which was waiting to be cleared for takeoff to Iowa City. Next to me sat a large young man who occupied his seat and a portion of mine. While the pilot warmed up the engines, Andrew and I talked. At six foot six and three hundred pounds, he was being recruited to play football for the Iowa Hawkeyes. I could understand why the university wanted such a large athlete to play defensive tackle. As we discussed sports, Andrew quietly confessed to me that his biggest fear was flying, not playing against the "big guys" on Saturdays. Seeing that he was nervous and agitated, I attempted to distract him by asking questions about football. I also candidly shared with him my fears related to living in a strange country as a coach for the Peace Corps. Becoming calmer myself, I started to review the events of that day.

Reflecting back, it had been quite an eventful day. I had taken an early flight from Los Angeles to O'Hare Field, Chicago. The flight was routine for the most part, except for the unusually heavy snowfall as we approached the Midwest. The snowfall had stranded airplanes at O'Hare. Consequently, my short stopover in Chicago became a grueling five-hour ordeal. I had, however, made my connecting flight to Iowa City with Ozark Airlines, which still used DC-3s for their domestic air flights.

After I had fastened my seatbelt, met Andrew, and calmed myself with thoughts of the day, I looked out the small window as we taxied down the runway. From my vantage point, I could see that the prop engine and the right wing were covered with a blanket of snow. After several minutes, the plane's two engines began to sputter in a desperate attempt to harmonize together. Under the burden of the heavy snow, the small plane seemed to groan in its desire to take off. Eventually, with what seemed like the help of some of passengers who were leaning forward as if they wanted to yell, "You can make it, you can make it!", the plane reached an altitude just above the power lines. It was at this point in the trip that the plane started bobbing in an up-and-down motion, like a cork riding on the surface of the ocean.

My sense that we were going to crash became more acute by a hand touching—no, grabbing—my left shoulder. Thinking it was the stewardess, I turned in the direction of the aisle, only to see a crazed look on Andrew's face next to mine as he gasped, "We are going to crash! We are doing to die!" Immediately following these alarming words, he used his mighty hands (that he would actually use later on the football field to ward off the block of an offensive lineman) to pull me to his bear-like chest as though I were a small child needing the comfort and security of his mother. Gathering all of my strength, I quickly pulled back, only to see a distorted face grimacing with fear, accentuated by narrow eyes and a quivering mouth, screaming, "Help! Help!" Finally, with the plane beginning to stabilize and with the help of a sympathetic stewardess, the young giant next to me settled down. I feebly attempted to assure him (and myself) that we would survive this journey.

In contrast to our panic, the short distance from O'Hare to Iowa City airport revealed a white blanket of peaceful snow covering farms and small towns. Sensing that we were close to our destination and that we would actually arrive safely, the relieved football player opened up to me, confessing his fear of flying and how this fear had all but shattered his hopes of playing collegiate football. When he was very young, his father had died in an airplane accident. His mother, who had to work several jobs just to support her six children, could not provide for their university education. So since Andrew was the youngest of the six, his only hope for educational support was to play football for the Hawkeyes.

Having cancelled previously reserved flights, Andrew had made a hard choice that day to fly to Iowa City by himself in an attempt to conquer his phobia of flying. After weathering the journey, Andrew straightened himself up in his seat as though he had won a battle, turned to me, shook my hand, and said, "Thank you. I hope I didn't hurt you," as he winked proudly. He beamed at me with a new confidence on his face and determination in his parting words: "Look for me on the football field. I will be playing for the Hawkeyes on Saturday afternoon." Four years later, he was selected first team all-American defensive tackle at Iowa University.

We arrived at Iowa City's airport a little shaken but none the worse from the experience. Andrew and I deplaned and walked toward the small terminal together, both realizing that our futures would be different since we had made some hard choices. I also could hear the lyrics to "Moon River" running through my mind. If this was an indication of how this Peace Corps experience was going to be, *bring it on!*

3

Peace Corps Training

Artist: Ross Miller

Like the receiver whose eyes are focused on the football, his heart pounding with excitement, and his stomach turning with anxiety, I couldn't wait for Peace Corps training to start on February 22, 1963. After breakfast in the quadrangle complex early the next day, we met university officials who escorted us to a general assembly room where Peace Corps officials from Washington, D.C., welcomed us.

Next on the orientation program was the introduction of each volunteer who, in turn, was given an opportunity to share his or her reasons for joining the Peace Corps. Some of the answers varied, but most of the volunteers wanted to serve our country by helping Indonesian athletes train for and compete in the Olympics.

Finally, we met Mr. Dave Burgess, a former career officer in the Foreign Service, who had been selected by Sargent Shriver to be our "boss." Officially, he was introduced as the director of the Peace Corps contingent to Indonesia. I was deeply impressed with Mr. Burgess's career background and his desire to head up a diplomatically important project in Indonesia. After he briefly shared his love of serving in the Diplomatic Corps, he then explained the importance of our specific Peace Corps mission, for as Indonesia emerged onto the world scene, she could either embrace democracy or be swallowed up by Red China. He stressed that even though our project's goal was to train Indonesian athletes for the 1964 Olympic Games, we were to be positive role models as young Americans and to provide a more positive image than depicted in the mass media or in the popular book *The Ugly American*. It was then that Mr. Burgess reminded us of the three major purposes of the Peace Corps, which are still goals for our young people who represent the United States overseas today:

- To provide opportunities for Indonesian people to meet Americans who were typical of our country, not the stereotypes seen in films and on television,
- To provide opportunities for Americans to meet Indonesians, to appreciate their culture and way of life, and
- To provide skills or services to help the Indonesian people. In our particular case, we were to coach Indonesian athletes for the Olympics.

Mr. Burgess stressed the importance of all three purposes for the total success of the project. In concluding, he stressed the importance of being volunteers who represented our country well, without the tarnish of the "ugly American."

We were then ready to start a three-month training program that would challenge us both mentally and physically. The intense training included:

Physical Education/coaching skills	144 hours
Teaching of English as a Second Language (although our contingent was trained as coaches, we still had some ESL training)	144 hours
Indonesian language study	284 hours
Area Studies – history, economic policies, and culture of Indonesia	100 hours
Health and Medical training	30 hours
Physical training and recreation	72 hours
Peace Corps orientation	20 hours

The most intense training focused on the study of Bahasa Indonesian five days a week, four hours per day. Groups of three volunteers were teamed with Indonesian instructors who came from various areas of Indonesia and from various levels of Indonesian society. Famous Indonesian athletes in track and basketball, police officers and magistrates, and government officials joined to enrich the training program. What an excellent group of trainers! Their knowledge of the language and their patient instruction produced results. To their credit, most of us were eventually able to teach and coach fluently in the Indonesian language. For the record, after fifty years, I am still fluent in the language, and I attribute this to the fine training we received and to the emphasis on fluency. It was a thrill for me when I returned to Indonesia in 2011 for six weeks and found myself comfortable and happy conversing with the gracious Indonesian people in their expressive language.

Social conventions and cultural expectations, although part of official training, were often learned quickest in daily life once we arrived in Indonesia, not in freezing Iowa. On one such occasion, a betjak driver in Palembang was my teacher. Waiting for customers and smoking clove cigarettes, a motley crew of betjak drivers would gather nightly around a large tree in a Palembang park near my "home." I would often go there to practice Bahasa and to eat *pisang goreng* (fried bananas). One particular night, I bought enough to share with the exhausted drivers. The first person I handed the *pisang goreng* on a banana leaf to was Bupati, an older, sinewy man with brown teeth, some missing. He wore the typical betjak driver hat, a straw version of a Dutch farmer's hat. Suddenly, he slapped my left hand, causing the *pisang goreng* to fall to the dirt. Reeling back in surprise, I quickly realized that I had served the gift with my left hand, the hand considered dirty and insulting in the Indonesian culture. To his *"Saya tidak mau, kotor!"* (No, I don't want it; it's dirty!), I responded, *"Maaf"* (I am sorry). Embarrassed, I bowed as I served him another pesan goring, this time with my right hand. I had learned my cultural lesson—a courtesy that should extend to all levels of society! And I had many more cultural lessons—some minor, perhaps even subtle—to learn if I was going to interact effectively with the people.

Back in Iowa, as winter gave way to spring, Peace Corps training had reached the halfway mark. The training staff decided that we needed a break to recharge our batteries for the last six weeks' stretch of intense language training and coaching techniques, followed by graduation. We were going to the famous Drake Relays! Since many of us had participated in track and would be coaching Indonesians in various track events, this was a thrilling surprise and a welcomed relief. The Drake Relays were so popular at that time throughout the United States that they became the first sporting event to be televised on ABC's *Wide World of Sports* in 1961.

Early on a Friday morning, we volunteers and our Indonesian language instructors boarded a yellow "vintage" bus headed for Des Moines, Iowa, two hours away. Perhaps the black cloud of ominous smoke emitting from the tailpipe foreshadowed events yet to happen. The terrain between Iowa City and Des Moines, void of the winter snow, revealed flat farmlands with a few rolling hills. However, our bus even had difficulty conquering these small hills. With each one, fumes would shoot from the pipe with gaseous explosions. And this continued for the next 120 miles! Somehow, we began to feel that this was a low-budget outing designed, yes, to give us a needed break, but to also save the Peace Corps dollars. Most of us attempted to be good sports about the condition of the bus and its obnoxious eruptions, chalking the whole experience up to the Peace Corps' design to toughen us up for the Indonesian transportation systems or to measure our ability to cope with harsh conditions. Don't tell me about today's athletes who travel gloriously on plush coaches to distant competitions!

We arrived in the afternoon at the once-beautiful entrance to the Iowan Hotel, also a "vintage," located in the low-rent district of Des

Moines. Vintage bus and vintage hotel! The hotel, once a beautiful three-story brick building that graced the skyline of Des Moines, was now a dilapidated building fighting for its existence. The first floor served as a reception area and a restaurant and bar. The second and third floors were single hotel rooms containing bare essentials—a simple double bed and a bathroom. The bed took up most of the main room. However, the third floor was for "extended stay" residents. It was the third floor that gave the hotel its less-than-acceptable reputation as a "flop house."

Dick Doughty, the tallest of the volunteers at six foot nine, and I were paired up, as were all the volunteers. To be honest, Dick and I spent the entire night battling to keep on our own side of the vintage double mattress, which sagged toward the middle. Whenever we did eventually fall asleep, one of us would gradually slide toward the center of the bed, colliding with the other, and shout, "I'm sorry! I'm sorry!" Neither Dick nor I were counting, but it must have happened at least ten times that night. In addition to the embarrassing mattress "tag" that we experienced, there was a ruckus outside the volunteers' room next to us when a crazed woman from the third floor was yelling and attempting to kick down their door.

Morning did not come too soon! After a hearty breakfast, "Old Faithful," our vintage bus, picked us up for the anticipated Drake Relays, which started like they have for many years, with colorful, creative floats circling the track. The track events started with the high school boys' 100-meter race. Then it was exciting to see some of our country's greatest collegiate track stars participating in various events. The year 1963 marked the last year for the football-throw event. It had replaced the javelin throw in 1942.

What could have been more fun than a full day of watching track events with friends who would soon be heading overseas to spread the "track fever"? As we headed back to the University of Iowa and the training program, we felt renewed vigor to complete the final six rigorous weeks that would sharpen and integrate our abilities to teach and coach while speaking in Bahasa Indonesian. Our expectations were high as we realized that in just a few short weeks we would actually be coaching Indonesian athletes. Only six more weeks of keeping our noses to the grindstone!

And then graduation day arrived on May 17, 1963. Of the 250 original applicants who applied for the Indonesian project and the nineteen who had reported for training, seventeen of us were in the graduating class honored to be the first group representing the United States in Indonesia.

As we proudly assembled for a graduation picture, it occurred to me what a privilege it was to be facing an exciting future with some of the finest young Americans I had ever met. Some had given up sports careers in response to President Kennedy's call to service. There was Dick Doughty, who had played on the UC Berkeley's collegiate national championship basketball team. George Larson had set long distance track records at the University of Oregon. Others had sacrificed teaching jobs and prestigious coaching positions in response to the call for American young people (and those young at heart) to make a difference in this world. Indonesia was a strategic country, an emerging country struggling to define itself in light of its history of Dutch colonialism, the occupation by Japanese forces in World War II, and the omnipresence of communism in much of Southeast Asia. For the Peace Corps volunteers, there was no promise of any financial reward in the future, but we were having a great time responding to a new drummer.

Expecting to head back to the dorm to pack up for the ten-day home leave, we were surprised to learn that we were leaving immediately for Washington, D.C., to meet President John F. Kennedy at the White House, followed by an invitation to Sargent Shriver's ranch in Maryland. Could this be real?

Peering out the windows of the bus as it followed the Potomac River, which was lined with blossoming cherry trees, I sat in awe as I took in my first view of Washington, D.C., our nation's capital. Yes, there was deep sense of pride and respect as I passed historic monuments that I had only heard of until then. The Washington and Lincoln Monuments, the Capitol building, the Pentagon, and finally the White House reminded us that this was our country's Athens, Rome, and London—the historical and governing heartbeat of the United States.

Dressed in our 1960's formal attire of dark suits, white shirts, and narrow ties and sporting crew cuts typical of that era, we entered the portico of the White House as guests of President John F. Kennedy, whose dream had made the Peace Corps a reality. In the Rose Garden, we found ourselves among state department officials, Indonesian instructors, consulate officials, and Peace Corps staff. Anticipating the President's arrival, my mind flashed back to his book *Pt. Boat 109.*

John F. Kennedy was commander of *PT Boat 109* in the South Pacific during World War II. The purposes of PT boats were to conduct nightly operations in order to impede heavy Japanese traffic attempting to resupply thousands of Japanese soldiers entrenched in the New Georgia-Rendova area and to give warning when Japanese warships came into the Blackett Strait from the Ferguson Passage to attack United States' forces in this strategic Pacific theater.

Late in the night of August 1, 1943, a Japanese destroyer, the *Amagui,* traveling at a relatively high speed (23 knots) unknowingly struck Kennedy's PT boat, shattering it in half, immediately killing two of the sailors. Catapulted into the dark waters, eleven of Kennedy's men survived, some severely injured. Kennedy was thrown into the cockpit of the boat, reinjuring his weak back. However, that did not stop him, for Kennedy spent hours in the water rescuing his men and getting them safely onto a small island nearby. Treading water for so many hours worsened his back injury, but his men were safe.

Because of his heroics that night, Kennedy was later awarded the Navy and Marine Corps Medal. He also received the Purple Heart for injuries sustained in the accident, injuries that plagued him the rest of his life. In fact, later in his life, Kennedy would have to get down on his knees rather than bend from his injured waist area in order to hug and play with his children, Caroline and "John-John."

My brief reflection of the *Pt. 109* history fading, I found myself looking into the face of President John F. Kennedy as we shook hands. Physically, he seemed taller and thinner than he appeared on television or in the newspapers. His eyes seemed tired and his face drawn. Looking back to this time in history, I can't help but wonder if the stress in his face reflected the Cuban Missile Crisis and his decision to take a firm stand, even at the risk of war, against the Soviet Union installing missiles in Cuba that were capable of reaching the US mainland.

Yes! I was shaking hands with President John F. Kennedy, also the author of *Profiles in Courage,* who himself regularly made hard decisions, and yet it was he who was congratulating us for our decision to serve our country and the people of Indonesia. As he mingled among us, I felt honored that he looked each of us in the eyes, shaking our hands and offering his personal interest and support. What an awesome experience! What an awesome memory! Little did we know at the time that we would be the last group of volunteers to meet the President before his assassination six months later on November 22, 1963.

After this momentous occasion, we joined the Director of the Peace Corps, Sargent Shriver, at his ranch near Baltimore, Maryland, for a barbeque and an afternoon of softball. Sargent Shriver (President Kennedy's brother-in-law, who married Eunice Kennedy, and the father of Maria

Shriver) warmly welcomed us to his home nestled in the lush, green, horse country of rural Maryland. Having left the formalities of the official White House reception far behind, Shriver took his coat and tie off, rolled up his shirt sleeves, and was ready to take on the opposing team in true Kennedy athletic style. The only outfield for our homerun hits was the pasture land for the horses that was surrounded by white spruce picket fencing. A fantastic afternoon! An inspiring man! Watching Sargent Shriver hit the ball, I was glad to be on his team.

What a grand conclusion to our training and an inspiring sendoff to Indonesia!

4

The World before Us

There at last! After three days of traveling halfway around the world to Indonesia, we finally touched down at Jakarta International Airport. To our shock, however, an angry crowd met us, shouting, "Peace Corps, go home!", "United States of America, go home!", and "Crush Malaysia!" Like angry vultures hovering above their prey, placards swayed, reinforcing the demands and cries of the mob.

As all seventeen volunteers escaped into an awaiting bus, we were shocked at the motley mob of communist youth. Dressed in ill-fitting military garb, they were "welcoming" us with rocks and debris thrown against the bus's windows as they flayed the vehicle's sides with sticks or whatever they could pick up. Why? How could this happen? Why hadn't the Peace Corps told us that a possible demonstration might be awaiting us in Jakarta? The Red Chinese had even published a book with our photographs and short biographies about each volunteer, claiming that we were American spies for the CIA. In addition, there was a propaganda film shown in East Java theaters warning the Indonesians against Western spies *(mata, mata)*. Ironically enough, we were told in Peace Corps training that volunteers would only be sent to countries that wanted them.

Yes, the government of Indonesia wanted us, but the increasingly militant communist party of Indonesia, the PKI, had no room for us in its methodical attack on Western ideas and institutions. The demonstration mounted against us at the Jakarta airport was just a precursor to the mounting unrest and violence of the time. This all culminated two years later on October 1, 1965, when the PKI attempted to take control of Sukarno's government by beheading six of the top eight military generals in an attempted military coup. The two generals who escaped rallied the military and enraged citizens against the communists. The blood-bath frenzy that resulted left over four hundred thousand Indonesians dead. Of course, not all were communists. The book *The Year of Living Dangerously* provides an account of the events leading up to the attempted coup. It was into this brewing milieu that we seventeen young, optimistic coaches landed on June 1, 1963, anxious to train athletes for the Olympic Games in Tokyo, only to be met by militant demonstrators.

As our bus pulled away from the airport with an armed military escort, *bang!* some of the more brazen demonstrators broke the bus's back window just behind me. Shards of glass shattered around us. I glanced over at one shocked Peace Corps coach whose raised, outstretched arms seemed to ask, "Why were we sent to this place where we thought they wanted us? Didn't President Kennedy and President Sukarno agree to the details of our coaching mission?" To the shouts of the demonstrators and the blare of the military police sirens, we left the teeming airport behind. What a welcome to Indonesia!

Eventually, we left the polluted, densely-populated city as we headed toward the extensive new Asian Games Sports Complex on the outskirts of Jakarta. The Soviet Union had helped to finance this complex for the 1962 Asian Games, an alternative to the Olympics. There were new sports fields, stadiums, dormitories, and even workers' villages. What an impressive show the Soviets had provided to woo Indonesia and other emerging countries in Southeast Asia to their ideology.

As we approached the massive wrought iron gates of the sports complex, I noticed a well-fortified machine gun nest off to one side. Further into the complex, I noticed yet another gun nest. "Certainly these are for our protection," I cautiously hoped. What more could we encounter?

We were exhausted from three days of airline flights, during which we had touched down in Hawaii, Japan, Hong Kong, Viet Nam, Thailand, and Singapore. And then, once we were in Indonesia, there had been the unexpected hostile welcome at the Jakarta airport. It all seemed like a bad dream.

Once inside the sports complex and its guarded gates, we still had another welcome awaiting us. This time, however, it was more cordial. The Indonesian Sports Ministry officials and the in-country Peace Corps staff awaited us with broad smiles, hearty handshakes, and food, food, food at a formal reception. It's no wonder that we wearily tossed our suits and ties on our luggage and easily fell asleep that night, many of us still holding on to the dreams of the world before us.

Our two-week orientation started early the next day with a jog through the villages surrounding the sport complexes. It was here that we would learn to live in this new land by brushing up on our Indonesian language, adjusting to the climate and the culture, and keeping physically fit. So began the morning run that became a daily routine. One can only imagine what the Indonesians must have thought seeing seventeen noisy Americans, one volunteer six foot nine, jogging through their villages, greeting their children, the elderly people, and the roadside vendors with *selamat pagi* (good morning) or a *pa kabar?* (How are you?). Some smiled and scratched their heads; others went about their daily routines, seemingly ignoring us but peeking sideways to take in the scene.

And just imagine what we seventeen young, jogging Americans thought as we passed through villages where daily life took on a community rhythm. Children played and bathed in muddy streams. Toddlers lolled in the morning sun as they played with sticks and rocks outside their small houses. We laughed as we passed children as young as five years old yanking on strings with kites attached as they tried to imitate their older brothers, who took kiting seriously. While the kites did not rise majestically, these little guys had all the moves down pat. Scrawny kampung dogs scrounged for scraps or slept everywhere, just as pesky flies also buzzed everywhere. Likewise, skinny, long-legged kampung chickens roamed freely. Men worked their gardens or rice fields. A solitary black bike leaning against a palm tree often indicated a man was working in his rice paddy. At noonday, women could be seen delicately maneuvering along the narrow mounds of dirt separating the rice fields to deliver lunches wrapped in banana leaves. Toothless old men gathered for their daily talk. Their clove cigarettes permeated their space, and the open sewers also permeated the village. Even the tropical trees and flowering vines seemed to join the community rhythm.

Returning from our run that first day, a bus awaited us for a tour of Jakarta, the nation's capital. We left the serenity of the outlying area, once again heading back to the crowded metropolis, which never slept.

The Peace Corps staff in Jakarta had arranged for us to tour the historic city. Naturally, the best place to start was at the heart of the city, Merdeka Square, around which the multilane one-way traffic jostled, hummed, and honked at all hours of the day and night. In the square, a national monument, popularly called the Monas, is a tribute to the first president of modern-day Indonesia, President Sukarno. Construction on the monument lasted from 1961 to 1975. Made of Italian marble, this monument is a bold, central column that originally soared higher than any other building in the city. It symbolizes the new Indonesia that was born out of the suffering of the people who revolted against European colonialism. Underground is a library and museum, and on top of the column, which rises 132 meters, a gold flame juts skyward.

The national museum boasts a treasure trove of cultural artifacts from throughout Indonesia. One section of special interest displays the costumes and model houses of the many ethnic groups comprising this three-thousand-mile-long archipelago nation. What a wonderful chance for us to begin to appreciate the culture and people with whom we would live for the next two years.

One important stop was the US Embassy, where we had to register. As we approached the embassy's large doors, two marines in dress uniforms welcomed each of us with a sharp salute. The American flag flying high above and occasionally snapping in the wind struck a patriotic chord deep within me. Yes, I was proud to be representing my country. Once inside the embassy, we took care of the official business and then gathered in the press room. When Ambassador Howard P. Jones stepped up to the lectern to welcome us officially, I again felt honored to be serving my country. Ambassador Jones, a career diplomat who spoke fluent Indonesian, thanked us for coming to Indonesia, where he had served for five years. I sensed he had a sincere interest in Indonesia and her people, and again I was proud to be numbered among the Americans there. Echoing President Kennedy's commitment to Indonesia as an ally, he stressed the importance of our sports mission and of establishing genuine relationships with the people.

The next day, after jogging and conditioning, we boarded the bus for a trip to the United States Information Service Library (USIS Library) in Jakarta. Since textbooks, reference books, and other reading materials in English were scarce, the United States helped university and secondary students by providing those much-needed educational materials. I was surprised by how much students were relying on the textbooks from the United States, especially those in math, science, and agriculture. The literature collection was extensive. It was at this same USIS library that I would later witness the burning of thousands of those books.

We never missed the early-morning run through the villages, often with gleeful children trailing after us like kite tails. Nor did we neglect the afternoon focus on language study in Bahasa Indonesian, either in a classroom or by chatting with the villagers. This routine became so common place that even the villagers expected us early each day.

One longer day trip took us to the beautiful city of Bogor, in the highlands located forty-seven kilometers south of Jakarta, a drive of about one and a half hours. At one thousand feet altitude, the cool air replaced the humidity of the capital, and the terraced rice fields replaced the stifling, crowded city. Bogor boasts magnificent botanical gardens covering eighty hectares (198 acres). There are streams and lotus ponds among the fifteen thousand species of trees. The orchid houses display three thousand varieties of orchids. The summer palace of President Sukarno was located in these gardens.

It was here that we were guests of Madame Hartini, the second wife of President Sukarno. We met her in her magnificent palace, which was surrounded by her personal, extensive, eighteenth-century gardens. Already in awe of the botanical gardens, we seventeen coaches were speechless as we entered Madame Hartini's palace and gathered to meet her. As she walked down the hall toward the "grand room," her natural beauty and grace distinguished this famous lady. She wore a traditional Indonesian sarong and silk blouse. Greeting each of us individually, Madame Hartini thanked us for coming to serve in Indonesia. One of the renowned ladies of Asia, this petite lady with shining eyes graciously made us feel welcomed, and we certainly felt honored to meet her.

Then ushering us into the grand room, we were seated for an official audience. The formal occasion dictated that we politely sit while the dignitaries, both Indonesian and American, exchanged greetings with one of the world's most influential women. The military guards and palace police encircled the room. Subdued and respectful, we seventeen coaches attempted to represent our country well. We certainly presented a different image than those seventeen joggers who laughed and shouted and engaged local villagers each morning just outside the Asian Games Complex.

It was during our orientation period that we received our coaching assignments. Most of us were to go in pairs to cities on the major islands of Java and Sumatra. Although Indonesia is the world's largest archipelago with islands stretching over three thousand miles, our Peace Corps focus was the populated islands of Java and Sumatra, which are located on the western edge of the archipelago. Jim Noonan and I were assigned to Palembang, South Sumatra. We were told that Palembang, a commercial city of seven hundred thousand people, had very little interest in competitive sports. Jim and I, however, immediately jumped at the challenge.

We began mapping out a strategy for a sports program that would awaken this commercial center. By developing track clinics at the various secondary schools in Palembang, we would open sports to all students and attract top athletes. An All-Palembang Junior Olympics would foster competition for spots on the Olympic team. We could even support the various sports by organizing a serious weight training program, using proven methods to strengthen all our Olympic-bound athletes. We hoped that publicized, thriving sports programs throughout Palembang would eventually draw enough attention from businesses and city leaders to possibly lead to local financial support. We would set foot in Palembang running, since we had specific goals and, of course, expected support from Indonesia's ministry of sports and the Peace Corps staff in the capital. The world ahead of us seemed full of possibilities.

The final day arrived when we coaches would leave Jakarta to begin our assignments throughout the country. It would not be easy to leave our friends after three months of intense training and orientation to live alone in this new country. However, this goodbye was also a chance for us to say hello to the towns and people we would come to serve.

As just Jim and I crossed the tarmac and anxiously boarded the small Garuda DC-3 airplane headed for Palembang, I took a determined, deep breath and said to him, "Well, buddy, Palembang, here we come, ready or not."

5

Palembang, Here We Come, Ready or Not

eaving the busy Jakarta airport behind, the DC-3 flew over the Sunda Strait, a narrow body of water separating Indonesia's large islands of Java and Sumatra. As we left Java, one of the most densely populated places on earth, we approached Sumatra, which is blanketed with some of the largest jungles on the earth. It hit me then that I was entering a strange new world. The plane followed the brown serpentine Musi River to the ancient and historic city of Palembang, soon to be my new home for two years. From the plane's window, the ships on the river—tankers, freighters, and houseboats—looked like matchsticks lying on the surface of the water, as though they had been strewn there by the hand of a mythological god.

Even before Palembang had a reputation as a major commercial center in Southeast Asia, it had a rich history. It was known in the seventh century as a Buddhist-studies center. In the eighth century, it was the site for a renowned Islamic university that attracted students from all over the Far East. In contrast to its commercial and religious status, however, there was no tradition of competitive sports. Little did Jim and I realize that a disinterest in sports would plague our efforts to organize programs and train athletes for the 1964 Olympic Games.

Finally, after a little more than an hour's flight, we arrived at Talang Betutu Airport, where we were graciously met by Major Askar, the head of the welcoming committee comprised of city and Ministry of Sports officials.

After the traditional Indonesian formalities, Jim and I were taken to Hotel Swarma Dwipa, which would be our temporary housing until KOGOR (the Ministry of Sports) could find us jobs and suitable accommodations with an Indonesian family. Months would pass, however, before Jim and I came to understand that the fanfare, although very impressive, carried empty promises.

In the afternoon of the day of our arrival, Jim and I were curious about our new surroundings and anxious to start acclimating. Making our way to the center of town, we walked along Sudirman Boulevard., where we marveled at the kaleidoscope of unique sights, smells, and sounds that seemed to collide, extending a discordant welcome to us. Chinese shops with living quarters in the rear lined the main dirt street. On both sides of that same main street, foul-smelling open sewers provided drainage. My mouth dropped when I saw an ice vendor dragging a huge block of ice up the muddy street. He would stop at various stores and restaurants to chop off smaller blocks, which would be used for refrigeration and for iced drinks. Sounds absorbed us into the Palembang scene. Horns blasting from impatient motorists, shouts from hawkers attempting to sell their wares, and bells ringing from betjak drivers joined to create our first impressions of Palembang. We walked as far as the docks along the Musi River, where again we were shocked at the standards of sanitation. Along that river, in the space of one hundred feet, we saw a person relieving himself, another washing lettuce, someone bathing, and a woman collecting a container of water. In contrast, Jakarta had been so new and romantic to us when we stayed in the impressive sports complex and visited the highlights of the capital, as if we were tourists. The realities of Palembang, however, hit both Jim and me hard, like a sudden slap in the face. Palembang put on no pretense for us. This different world would be our world for two years, and the first months of adjustment and settling in lay immediately before us.

Early in the evening of the first day, we had tea with Major Askar, who seemed open to and supportive of our plan to initiate a multi-pronged sports program in Palembang. I did sense, however, that we had much to learn from these fine people if we were going to be effective. The programs, the training, and the emphasis would have to be theirs, not our American plan for them. Because of Palembang's history and economic priorities, we would probably be facing an uphill battle. Nevertheless, Jim and I were both optimistic and committed to working alongside the people after our meeting with Major Askar.

It didn't take long for homesickness and discouragement to creep up on me as I went to bed each night those first few weeks. While we were struggling to settle in, missionaries Bob and Pat Gonia showed up at Hotel Swarma Dwipa to introduce themselves and to offer us help in acclimating to the living conditions and culture of Palembang. Many times they came to our rescue by providing warm hospitality with lunches, dinners, game nights, rides, and introductions to new Indonesian friends to ease the pain of homesickness and frustration. Their encouragement was like a ship's rudder keeping us on course. Bob always had an encouraging word for us, a generous spirit, and availability to drive us anywhere at any time, such as when he used his truck to pick up our lost luggage from the airport.

Bob even showed me how to survive the antiquated postal system. I will never forget going with him to the local post office to mail some letters back home. What a bureaucratic process just to mail a letter! First, we stood in a long line to weigh each letter. Next, we joined another longer line to get the appropriate stamps. And then we stood in the last line, the longest, to send the letters. To call it a *line* is a stretch of the imagination. The process just to mail letters could take hours, so I was grateful to Bob and his patient introduction to yet another cultural experience.

During this time of uncertainty and adjustment, Jim and I knew that by not having coaching jobs, we could easily become discouraged. We made an agreement to get up each morning and shave and take a shower. We would greet each day with a positive attitude; after all, weren't we "two drifters off to see the world"? Well, sometimes the day didn't realistically start this way, but at least we were determined to try.

Along with adjusting to new demands and surroundings, Jim and I both came down with severe cases of Palembang dysentery. For several long days and nights, we played "toilet tag." When Jim wasn't on the toilet, I was. After one of my dashes to the toilet, Jim shouted in clear coaching fashion, "Paul, I think you just broke the two-meter sprint record." I had never been so sick in my life. I didn't even have the strength to get dressed or even to eat. While we were lying in our twin beds, too sick to move, we watched in speechless disbelief as the hotel housekeeper cleaned the dirty toilet bowl with a soiled rag and then, without much pause in the action, used the same disgusting rag to clean our drinking glasses on a nearby table. There was not any question why we were both ill. In a desperate attempt to save what remained of our lives, I said to the hotel housekeeper, *"Tidak baik! Tidak baik!"* (Not good! Not good!). Then, with a quick, feeble demonstration, I attempted to explain to him basic sanitation by throwing the foul rag into the garbage can. It is a wonder that the rag didn't crawl out of there on its own. We were too sick to be mad at our situation and didn't even have the means to contact anyone for help.

And then we were robbed! Repeatedly! Because of the humidity and our sickness, it was necessary for us to hand wash our clothes frequently. We hung them up to dry in a private, enclosed area outside our room before we left the hotel each morning. We felt secure because of the jagged, broken glass cemented to the top of the surrounding tall wall. Many evenings when we returned, however, we discovered that we had literally been "pantsed." An underwear thief was stealing our clothes off the line.

In addition to clothing, Jim's keepsake class ring came up missing, and someone made off with several thousand rupiahs, right under our noses while we were sleeping. We even began to wonder if we were being lulled into a deep sleep by sleeping powder blown into our room during the night. There were rumors that robbers would place long bamboo sticks filled with sleeping powder under a door, blow the potion into the room, and then wait for their victims to fall asleep. In our desperation to stop the thievery, we decided to stay up all night and lay a trap for our robber. Just in case we might fall asleep, we put our own powder—baby powder!—on the floor so that we could track the footsteps to determine from which direction the thief was entering. As "luck" would have it, we fell asleep that night, only to discover the next morning that we had been robbed again. Footprints in the powder revealed that the thief had boldly entered our room by way of our locked door. After carefully presenting the evidence to the manager of the hotel, he expressed his feelings of regret, promised to do all he could to retrieve the lost items, and we never heard from him again.

When we had arrived in Palembang a month before, we were told that the Hotel Swarma Dwipa would be our temporary housing until the KOGOR could find us suitable accommodations with an Indonesian family. Often, it is the host family that is the key to a Peace Corps volunteer's adjustment. Living with a family opens the door to that country's language and its culture. Jim and I continued to ask ourselves why no one had followed through with the housing or job commitment. What was going on?

Fifty years later, as I was preparing to write this memoir, the answers became clear. I managed to make contact with Alex Shakow, who had been the in-country director of our Peace Corps project and who offered to send the complete files that he had kept on me from 1963–1965. Alex's knowledge of the language and his prior experience in Indonesia certainly qualified him to coordinate our projects. He worked out of Jakarta but regularly traveled throughout Sumatra and Java visiting the volunteers, encouraging, and "putting out fires." But back to the questions that were gnawing at Jim and me our first lonely month in Indonesia, why? What was going on?

After reading the files, one part of the puzzle became clear. We had not heard from anyone—at the local or national level—because of a "misdirected radiogram." Prior to our arrival, that radiogram had been sent to the authorities in Palembang, requesting their attendance at an important planning meeting in the capital to finalize details and housing related to our job assignments. That radiogram never arrived. No Palembang sports representatives went to that meeting in Jakarta, and consequently no one in Palembang knew what to do with us once we arrived there. So without realizing the dynamics at play, Jim and I were basically drifting on our own for our first month. We were floundering, with no coaching jobs and living in little more than a shabby hotel where we became sick and were robbed.

Additionally, there were various reasons why the citizens and leaders of Palembang were reluctant to welcome us into their homes and limited sports programs. There seemed to be a great hesitancy on the part of the citizens to accept responsibility for providing lodging and hospitality to two American Peace Corps volunteers. Some citizens had apprehensions that they could not meet the living standards most foreigners demanded. Again, communication had broken down. Not enough information had been provided to Palembang's city officials about the purpose and principles of the Peace Corps. We were not just American visitors. The city officials did not understand that this American program specifically stated that volunteers would speak the language and live at the same standards as their host counterparts—in our case, coaches and teachers.

Finally, some families were fearful of the political consequences of having any connections with the United States. Our arrival in Indonesia came at a time when there was political tension between Indonesia and the United States over Viet Nam, and between Indonesia and Britain over Britain's involvement in Malaysia. In addition, we arrived there a couple of years prior to the attempted communist coup, so there was much internal tension going on under the surface of daily life and politics. For whatever reasons, there were influential citizens who were reluctant or afraid to speak out or act on our behalf. Jim and I continued to question why officials had readily entered government agreements to host Peace Corps volunteers (and accepted the resulting US monetary aide to Indonesia) yet failed to provide coaching jobs. As the reasons for the breakdown in communication became evident, positive changes slowly began.

Eventually, Mr. Bahar, a civil servant working for the KOGOR, found out about our living conditions and offered us temporary lodging in his small two-bedroom house. He emphasized that this was a temporary arrangement, but it lasted for three months. His decision to accept us into his home was *berani* (courageous), in light of the fact that certain circles in Palembang society strongly opposed our presence there. Jim and I were humbled by Mr. Bahar's hospitality, especially considering that many of the officials, who publically welcomed us on our arrival in Palembang, had larger homes and more financial means. Their welcome mats had been withdrawn, and yet the Barhars sincerely welcomed us into their family.

And, yes, it was a rich experience living with Pak and Ibu (respectful terms for "father" and "mother") and their six children, ranging in age from six to nineteen years old. Although our rent may have brought some additional income, Pak and Ibu's offer of hospitality must have put tremendous pressure on their family. Pak and Ibu crammed all six of their children into their bedroom. Jim and I were given the second bedroom. We certainly had no complaints. All we had to cram under our twin beds was our luggage, sports equipment, and what was left of our clothing after the repeated robberies in the hotel.

Next to our bedroom was the family bathroom, a small, windowless room with tile flooring. The toilet was a typical Indonesian toilet, consisting of two bricks on either side of a drain hole. On one side of the bathroom were a water basin and a tin bucket, which I used to pour cold water over my head for a shower, known as "taking a *mandi.*" We had never practiced taking a mandi during Peace Corps training, but it didn't take us long to catch on. Nevertheless, after a sweltering night, it was often invigorating to greet the day by taking a mandi in my Indonesian home and saying to myself, "Good morning, Mr. Paul." I was beginning to feel that there was hope.

The best part of being in the Bahar family was mealtime around the rugged, wood family table. Ibu would prepare traditional Indonesian dishes. We usually had strong coffee in the morning, so strong that it seemed as if the spoon would stand straight up in the coffee cup. Bread and jam, a carryover from the Dutch colonial times, would accompany the coffee. Occasionally we would have *nasi goreng* (fried rice) for breakfast. That same fried rice would be served for lunch and even dinner that same day. Fruit, which was served at every meal, often included delicious Sumatran pineapple. After meals, there were warm times when the children would linger around the table, chatting curiously and sometimes practicing their limited English with us. This seemed to please Pak Bahar since he wanted his children around us. The times when Jim and I sang songs for the children brought squeals of delight. Their favorite song was "Old MacDonald Had a Farm," even with the older children. "Sing it again! Sing it again!" echoed, especially when we made the animal sounds.

In addition to providing room and board, Ibu washed our clothes. Since she did not have a modern washing machine, she would join other women at a nearby river, where she would hand wash our clothes (and those of her own family) by using a rock and soap to pound and scrub them clean. Without a mechanical agitator, her scrub rock did the job just fine. The process, however, did result in chipped buttons and zippers that refused to zip. At that time, most of the water from the rivers in Indonesia was not potable. It was not fit to drink. Cleaning white clothes in brown, polluted rivers meant that our clothes often took on a tan hue. Missionaries later told us that prominent citizens of Palembang had complained about our lack of cleanliness. Those opinions did not faze us; we were living and thriving in the Bahar family under Ibu's care.

Jim and I had an ongoing battle, in fact, a herculean battle, with cockroaches that never ceased. Nighttime was the worst. Since there was not any electricity at night, we would carry a candle, along with a stick, each time we dared to enter the bathroom. Opening the door first, I would peek in to scout out what was awaiting me. Often I would find the entire bathroom floor swarming with cockroaches, with more of their comrades oozing out of the toilet hole. It seemed an endless siege! We often lost count of the number of cockroaches we killed each night. Hundreds! *Hundreds!* If we weren't fighting them on the bathroom home turf, we were swatting them off our faces as we tried to sleep. In spite of all this, we felt the satisfaction of being part of a family and connecting with other people living in our *kampung,* a poor neighborhood enclave within a larger city.

The ongoing struggle to find coaching jobs continued for several more months. Even though Jim and I did conduct track clinics occasionally and did some volleyball coaching, there was little interest in developing an extensive sports program in Palembang. We were losing hope. We had arrived five months previously with high expectations and an attitude of "ready or not." Palembang, in fact, was not ready for us. Jim eventually put in a request for a transfer to Medan, where he helped to develop a thriving track program. Mission accomplished! Fifty years later, Jim is still involved in track. He recently won the pole vault event in a masters' meet in Minnesota.

It was during this period of struggling for coaching jobs that I was offered a job teaching English at the University of Sriwidjaja, one of the oldest universities in Indonesia. Although I was sent to Indonesia as a track coach, I held a degree in English and had taught English and coached at the secondary level in California. The open door to teach was a fantastic opportunity to interact with young people and to use another set of my skills and interests. Preparing lessons and lecture notes and delving into literature certainly gave me a purpose, the exact antidote I needed to ward off discouragement and to jumpstart two worthwhile years in Indonesia.

Yes, the Peace Corps would later move me to more spacious accommodations, with a housekeeper. I would leave the kampung for a better neighborhood. The roads were even paved. My clothes were cleaner. And the cockroaches became a memory of the past. I would find much fulfillment teaching and interacting with students at the university and on the athletic fields. I was never more happy in Indonesia, however, than when I lived with the loving, welcoming Bahar family.

6

Teaching at University of Sriwidjaja

On February 3, 2011, I turned seventy-one years old while teaching, once again, in Indonesia, this time at Bandung Alliance International School. It was appropriate that as a teacher of English I would finish my teaching career where I started it fifty years previously, in Indonesia. Those fifty years held adventures both in the realms of literature itself and in "kingdoms" around the world. Teaching and studying in the United States, Kenya, Scotland, and Indonesia was awesome. And the added thrill came when I enjoyed the adventures with my wife and three children.

It was January 2011 when my wife, Marilyn, and I enjoyed walking side by side to school each day in Bandung, Indonesia. This time as a team, I taught English classes and she worked on English as a Second Language (ESL) curriculum. I was back in Indonesia! And she was back in the land I had talked about for so long, so long that she seemed to know it instinctively. When friends or even strangers offered us rides to the school in their cars or on motorbikes, we politely declined. The daily walk to school was so rich in scenery, sights, sounds, and memories that we kept our daily walks just for ourselves. Among the many conversations, we talked about teaching memories. No greater honor could satisfy my soul than to recall immersing my students and myself in the treasures of writers who challenge all of us to consider who we are and what we are doing with ourselves. Those rewarding times included the two years with fine Indonesian students as we also delved into the realms of literature.

Back in 1963, our Peace Corps contingent of seventeen coaches eagerly anticipated our assignments coaching and teaching Indonesian athletes for the 1964 Olympic Games in Tokyo, Japan. When I arrived in Palembang, however, to discover that no definite coaching assignment awaited me, flexibility and patience were necessary. In fact, within several months it became clear to us that Indonesia was withdrawing from the Olympic Games and joining in the New Emerging Forces Games, a sports competition organized for communist countries. I was without a full-time coaching job!

At the same time in 1963, the University of Sriwidjaja was in the process of initiating a new English-speaking program for its FKIP students, people who planned to teach English at the secondary level. Professor Domes was returning to New Zealand, so the FKIP department needed another English teacher to fill his position. It had to be more than luck that this teaching opportunity came right at a time when coaching jobs for me were not materializing in Palembang. I still do not know to this day how the university obtained my name and knew my academic background in English. However, it happened. I was offered the job, and I felt so grateful for the opportunity to teach English literature and ESL at the University of Sriwidjaja.

Since I would be teaching English eighteen hours a week, mornings, as a full-time professor, I would still have the opportunity to coach track and conduct coaching clinics in the afternoons for KOGOR, the sports ministry in Palembang. This combination of responsibilities would allow me to fulfill my coaching duties to the Peace Corps and still teach English for the university. Alex Shakow, our in-country director, excitedly supported my decision to accept the English position. He saw it as an opening door for Peace Corps volunteers to teach at the university level. And the university administrators were thrilled that I was joining the English faculty. When Alex reminded me that I could not accept a salary, Dr. Hardjono (the rektor-president of the university) and I worked out a plan to use the money to pay the driver of the school truck to pick up other teachers needing transportation to the university. That also included me. It was a win-win situation.

The only people who seemed disgruntled about my teaching assignment were the young communists of the PKI, the highly organized Communist Party of Indonesia. In fact, by 1965, Indonesian communists boasted the largest party membership outside of Russia and China. Frankly, they nearly came unglued at the prospect of an American teaching at one of their top universities. So much for tolerance of diverse thought!

It was shortly after I started teaching at the university that the PKI stepped up its propaganda machine against the Unites States' military involvement in Viet Nam and the Peace Corps' presence in Indonesia. Obviously, they did not know (or want to know) that Kennedy's Peace Corps concept focused on service through people to people contact. Our training program in Iowa had emphasized that we were not to become involved in politics. Additionally, the United States Information Service (USIS) libraries were closed throughout Indonesia because the PKI opposed what they considered the spread of Western ideas in Indonesian universities. In fact, I witnessed a PKI mob burning books after it had gutted the USIS library in Jakarta. A mountain of books from the world's greatest literature was set aflame with singed pages of Plato, Hugo, Shakespeare, and T. S. Eliot wafting in the air above the heads of the young communist yelling, "Down with Western ideas! Crush Malaysia, and crush the British and American imperialists!" Strangely, I felt as if I were standing alongside Ray Bradbury as he described the book burnings in *Fahrenheit 451*. Scenes of this misdirected hatred are vividly portrayed in the book (and movie), *The Year of Living Dangerously,* by Christopher Koch. Eventually, the pressure from the communists caused the closure of all USIS libraries throughout Indonesia. Consequently, thousands of secondary and university students were unable to prepare for their final examinations without the use of these books and reference materials.

It was several days after a large communist demonstration in Jakarta while I was shopping in Palembang that I was approached by several dubious-looking characters whom I had never seen before. They discreetly approached me with a quiet, ominous warning to "leave the university—or else." At this time, I dismissed the threat as only a scare tactic. I felt keenly that I was doing well with my classes. My mind went immediately to a Bible verse I had memorized as a child: "For I know the plans I have for you, declares the Lord, plans to prosper you and not to harm you, plans to give you hope and a future" (Jeremiah 29:11, NIV). I thought that was the end of their harassment of me, but there was more to come. The communist agenda for the overthrow of the existing Indonesian leaders was fomenting at a fast pace, as the world would realize only two years later in the attempted coup.

Back at the University of Sriwidjaja, between 1963 and 1965, I continued to immerse myself teaching and enjoying my English courses and students. When the PKI would rattle their swords against the United States or the Peace Corps, my students would often graciously warn, "Mr. Paul, stay inside, please. There are demonstrations today." And Rektor Hardjono heartily continued to support my teaching in spite of opposition.

I still recall my first day of teaching at the university. My stomach was turning nervously and my mouth was dry. I kept thinking of demonstrators who had carried banners demanding, "Kick the Peace Corps out of Indonesia!" In fact, once when I was heading toward the university, I even spotted my name on a placard: "Kick Paul out of Indonesia!" Such opposition brought out my strength and determination to do the best job of teaching English literature (not Western ideologies or politics) for my students. I was not a spy for the United States, as some suggested. I was not a CIA agent. I was not even a professor who attempts to teach a biased interpretation of literature. As I approached my classroom, I finally took courage in the knowledge that I was a twenty-three-year-old American who graduated with a degree in literature and who longed to share the inspiration, beauty, and challenges that great writers of all ages have gifted to the world. When I entered the lecture hall, several students bashfully smiled and opened the double doors for me. In polite Asian style, all the students stood to welcome me. I couldn't believe their gracious reception. I still, however, had much to learn! Encouraged by their respect and thirst for education, I asked them to take their seats and open up their notebooks. Right away, they eagerly took notes on "The Beginnings of English Literature," the syllabus that would guide our first semester. So began two memorable years of teaching.

From the start, I knew I had two different challenges to overcome in order to be an effective teacher at the university. First, I was an American living in a country that was becoming more anti-American daily, fueled, probably, by the American involvement in Viet Nam. The other problem, perhaps somewhat superficial, was my age. I had graduated in 1962 with a B.A. in English and history and was working on my M.A. I had been coaching American football since 1961. Since Indonesian culture holds older people in high esteem, at twenty-three I had many years to go before I met the cultural qualifications for respect. "Perhaps," I hoped, "the way I conduct my classes and the content will bring respect from my students."

At the end of the first and second weeks, I sensed we were off to a good start. Eager students participated in class discussions, and of course, there was never a doubt that homework was completed well. I thoroughly enjoyed class discussions, often sparked by thoughtful questions, which showed that my students were not only understanding the literature but interacting and questioning it. Anyone who has taught knows that I am describing a truly rewarding teaching experience. When many students even stayed after class for additional help, I decided to offer English tutorials on Saturday mornings. To my surprise, every student in the class came for the extra help. It was very clear that, in Indonesia, an education could mean the difference between merely eking out an existence and success. I must admit, however, that dear Omar in my beginning ESL class still needed much practice with basic terms, such as *good morning* and *good evening.*

Then with the third week came an unexpected turn. These same eager students seemed distracted and even reluctant to participate in class. I could tell by their eyes that something was wrong, something was bothering them. Indonesia, like many other Asian countries, has a saying that the eyes are the windows of the soul. So I quietly asked two of my better students, Armen and Sri, to stay after class, and even they came forward with their heads down and no eye contact. When I asked them if there was a problem, they responded with a sheepish, embarrassed response: "Mr. Paul, we like you as an instructor, but the communists are putting pressure on us not to attend your classes because you are an American and belong to the Peace Corps."

This time I firmly explained my purpose for teaching them: "I am teaching English literature, not American Studies. In the past two weeks, have I said anything political or made any comments against Indonesia?"

"No," they honestly responded. "How long will you be teaching at our university?"

"Rektor Hardjono has asked me to teach at least three semesters. I want you to know that I sincerely enjoy teaching here. I feel this class is bright, responsive, and capable of handling the course work. I am here to stay."

"Well, the communists say that you do not care about us and that you will be leaving soon. Do you think we could do some activities outside of school to get to know you and to practice our English?"

"Of course!" I responded.

"Mr. Paul, we want you to care for us not only as Indonesian students but as people as well."

Wow! The door was open for building positive relationships *and* reinforcing English skills through conversation. From the start, I had felt an affinity for these students, even though some were older than I was, and now they were reaching out to me! During the remaining terms, I would be privileged to attend their weddings and special celebrations. We would continue the Saturday tutorials and take occasional field trips.

In fact, at the next class session, I surprised them by announcing that the class would have a picnic off campus the following Friday after the 11:45 a.m. lecture. It was obvious from their burst of joyous chatter that they were excited that I wanted to do something with them. When Sri and Armen volunteered to organize the picnic, others eagerly joined the planning committee. The tension in the classroom had melted and classes went well for the rest of the week. Once again, my students' beautiful faces and bright, brown eyes reflected smiles from their hearts.

At last, Friday afternoon arrived, and after meeting on the lawn at the front of the administration building, we started our walk to a local park. Along the way, there were laughs and chatter, and eventually the students broke out into well-known Indonesian songs such as the patriotic song,

"Hallo Hallo Bandung":

(Bahasa Indonesian)	(English)
Hallo, hallo Bandung	Hallo, hallo Bandung
Ibukota Periangan	Capital city of Priangan
Hallo hallo Bundung	Hallo hallo Bandung
Kota kenang-kenangan	City of many memories
Sudah lama beta	It's been so long
Tidak berjumpa dengan kau	Since I met you
Sekarang telah menjadi lautan api	Now burning like a sea of fire
Mari bung rebut kembali	Let's go take Bandung back.

The children's song "Gelang Sipaku Gelang" was
my favorite, one that I still remember:

(Bahasa Indonesian)	(English)
Gelang sipaku gelang	Walking home happily
Gelang si rama rama	like fluttering butterflies

Mari pulang	Let's go home
Marilah pulag	Come, let's go home
Marilah pulang	Come, let's go home
Bersama-sama	Together.

Mari pulang	Let's go home
Marilah pulang	Come, let's go home
Marilah pulang	Come, let's go home
Bersama-sama	Together

Within twenty minutes, we reached a beautiful park of well-manicured grass surrounded by palm trees. What a contrast to the busy academic grounds boasting well-manicured dirt. A few colorful blankets and sarongs were placed on the grass for the food, which consisted of fried rice (nasi goreng), chicken sate, shrimp crackers, and Sumatran fruits of all kinds. Cold tea and cookies followed for dessert. Thanks to the hospitable young ladies, we were well fed! It was a wonderful bonding time, so much so that there were calls for a group photo, one that I still treasure in my keepsakes.

During the picnic, however, my stomach was still acting up from a tenacious case of dysentery, not related at all to our wonderful picnic that day. Feeling the "call of nature," I asked, *"Dimana kamar kecil?"* (Where is the toilet?). The students laughed as they pointed to a stream. With no other choice and with nature still calling, I exited in the direction they were pointing. To my horror, the path led to a small, torpid stream in a clearing surrounded by dense jungle. "At least," I thought, "there is some privacy!" To be honest, I smelled the toilet before I saw it.

At a narrow part of the stream was a rickety board that spanned the stream from bank to bank. This board served as the toilet seat or toilet stand. If the smell was bad, the surrounding sight was even worse. Brown and green excrement lined both sides of the stream with yellowish-green foam bubbling on the surface. There is a Peace Corps motto: try anything once, and if it doesn't work out, never try it again. Taking this to heart, I squatted down on the board in my best Asian style—only to hear the worst sound in my life. The board cracked in half, catapulting me backward, up to my chin in their toilet.

My scream of "Oh, *sh*—!" brought my students to the edge of the stream to see their teacher attempting to keep his head above the muck in their toilet! Well, of course, they burst into laughter, shouting *"Lucu! Lucu!"*

37

(Funny! Funny!). as they saw me gagging for fresh air. Retching from the foul smells, I attempted to crawl out on the riverbank like a muddied creature from the black lagoon. How many students worldwide have had the comic pleasure of finding their teacher scrambling to survive in a toilet? Since there were no "helping hands," I used the jungle vines to bring me to safety. I am not sure if my trousers were up or down at that point! In any case, I reached the riverbank. My students caught up with me as I was attempting to clean myself up with leaves and sticks from the jungle. Their uncontrollable laughter lessened as they tried to help me by bringing whatever they could find—paper bags and lunch wrappings—to finish the cleanup job. It was fortunate that we had eaten lunch before I took my plunge!

Needless to say, there was much prolonged laughter at my expense. And to be honest, I laughed heartily, too. The way I had handled the messy situation spoke loudly to my students. Their empathy also spoke volumes to me. The trek back to the campus found us all, Indonesians and American alike, happy to have shared a picnic, music, our common humanity, and an afternoon together. This was a crucial turning point.

Several weeks later, when I spotted one of my students on Sudirman Boulevard in Palembang, he introduced me to his friend. As I left, I saw my student demonstrating to the other how I had fallen into the polluted stream toilet up to my chin. As they held their sides in laughter, crying, "Poor Mr. Paul," I knew the ice had been broken and that I was beginning to establish meaningful relationships with my students, in spite of the social unrest and political pressure from without. I had gone through my crucible during my initial months in Indonesia; now I had survived my "baptism."

Chapter 7
Visitors from Jakarta

Perhaps a Peace Corps volunteer's greatest dread, and yet perhaps his greatest joy, was both the scheduled and impromptu visits from the Peace Corps' in-country directors from Jakarta. I have heard horror stories from volunteers from all over the world detailing how the lack of representation and support from their in-country directors greatly impacted their effectiveness. Even though Jim and I had a difficult time initially finding jobs and housing in Palembang, the fault did not lie directly with Dave Burgess or Alex Shakow, our in-country directors. As mentioned previously, the KOGOR was not prepared for our arrival in Palembang, and this translated into no prearranged housing or jobs. (One wonders, at times, if host countries welcome the US aid in terms of cancelled debts but not the actual eager volunteers who want to impact their world.) We were the first Peace Corps contingency to arrive in Indonesia in 1963, and that meant adjustment for the volunteers, the Peace Corps in-country directors, and the host nationals. In fact, there was much to learn about patience and cultural differences between the Indonesians and us. Dave and Alex, however, did much to bridge these differences. Alex would travel across Indonesia checking on the volunteers throughout Sumatra and Java. He would arrive with his infectious smile, letters from home, and needed encouragement as he attempted to put out fires springing from homesickness, illness, cultural differences, and communication problems. The early contingents of Peace Corps volunteers actually lived and worked without cell phones (perhaps to their benefit). Letters from home could take months to arrive.

Three months after our arrival in Palembang, Alex came to check on our progress in establishing a sports program and a physical fitness testing program for South Sumatra. Alex's ability to speak Bahasa Indonesian and to relate culturally to the Indonesians helped us to initiate these two programs. Palembang was historically a trading and commercial city, so sports seemed of little importance.

For me, it was also a source of encouragement when Alex confirmed the importance of my teaching at the University of Sriwidjaja while I still worked with the KOGOR. Excerpts from a letter (dated March 25, 1964) that I received from Alex exemplify the support directors can provide:

"Paul, I want to compliment you again on the marvelous rapport you have at the university. It is terrific, and without question they are enjoying your assistance as much as—if not more than—you take delight in teaching there. There is no reason whatsoever that Soedino (sports program administrator) should not respond in the same way if you give a little time to it; with both of you at work up there, I anticipate great strides on all the Palembang fronts, also remembering that great strides in Palembang may appear small in comparison with other places but are major accomplishments in your town. Keep us fully posted on developments as I am particularly interested in seeing what you can create in what everyone agrees is a tough situation."

Alex also was instrumental in acquiring Ducati 50cc motorbikes for us to use in our work. This meant that we no longer had to rely on our feet or public transportation to get us to coaching clinics or to teaching responsibilities. No more half-hour breaks under thrashing palm trees while I waited out sudden tropical storms before I continued walking to a coaching commitment.

Since the roads always became worse during the wet season, our bikes were starting to break down because of use and the notorious potholes. I asked Alex to check them out when he next came to Palembang.

Fortunately, Alex was able to stop for several days on his way to Medan. After his arrival, Alex took a mandi, and we had the daily fare of fried rice, fruit, and pineapple juice. Of course, he knew that whatever rice was left over from breakfast would appear for lunch, minus the breakfast egg on top. For dinner, that same rice would appear as stir-fry, possibly with chicken or "mystery meat," as we called whatever we could not identify.

After lunch, Alex and I turned our attention to problems with the motorbike. The jump starter seemed to be faulty, which required that I run, holding onto the handlebars with the left hand while using the right hand to open the throttle, to start the bike. However, if one allowed too much throttle, the bike would tear out like a charging elephant, leaving the potential rider holding on for his dear life. I carefully explained this mechanical difficulty to Alex, and being the helpful person that he was, he responded with, "Paul, let me try." Pointing out to him that there was a reason for my limp and bandaged ankle, I warned him about the idiosyncrasies of the bike. In an attempt to protect Alex from a similar fate, I stood in front of the bike. But in full stride, Alex confidently grasped the handlebars, faked to his left, and then he went full speed to his right with the determination of a crazed man on a mission. A second later, I heard the bike's motor rev up to full speed with a screeching whine as it charged forward with Alex still attempting to straddle the seat. Fifty feet later, the victorious bike dumped Alex into thorny bougainvillea bushes along the dirt road where the cloud of dust soon began to settle. I rushed quickly to Alex's help, only to find him slightly shaken up by the experience. After a few pensive moments, a smile finally broke out on his face as he shouted, "I'm okay! But, Burghdorf, be careful! That bike wants to kill someone!"

With a few scratches on his face and arms, Alex said farewell to me at the airport, as I smiled, yelling, "Come back when you can spend more time!" I noticed that Alex did not glance back with a cordial response to my farewell, but he waved into the air with his good arm and limped to the DC-3 waiting to take him on to Medan.

Another guest whose visit left lasting impressions was a woman named Lilly from the State Department, who was doing research on the living conditions of Peace Corps volunteers throughout the world and how these conditions affected the volunteer's success in the field. Lilly had landed at Palembang Airport, and on her own initiative had taken a taxi to my house. The only notification of her visit was a startling knock on the front door, followed by her brashly introducing herself to my reserved host, General Soebutu, a retired army general who had fought courageously against the Japanese during WWII and subsequently against the Dutch for Indonesia's independence in 1948. (Jim and I had moved into the general's home when Pak Bahar had found more permanent housing for us.)

Lilly was provided a small bedroom down the hallway from mine. Between her bedroom and mine was the typical Indonesian bathroom. As a reminder to the reader, the Indonesian toilet consists of two raised bricks and a hole in the center. One usually squats over the toilet hole, being careful not to slip. No toilet paper is used; instead, water and the notoriously dirty left hand do the trick. In the same room, across from the two bricks and the hole was a mandi, a cement water basin about two feet by three feet that was filled with cold water, with a tin bucket floating on the water. This basin was the source of bath water for the entire family for the week. For a bath, a person would stand on the tile next to the basin, scoop a bucket of water from the basin, pour it over one's head, lather up, and then rinse from another bucket of water, and all that would run down to a drain at the center of the bathroom, and then out to the garden.

This long-standing bathing system of Indonesia was popularly known as "taking a mandi." In fact, it was so common that when greeting others walking along the street, friends would say, *"Sudah mandi?"* (Have you taken a bath?) just as Westerners say, "How are you today?" Initially, I remember being somewhat offended that strangers would want to know if I had taken a bath. After a few months, however, I had no qualms answering their questions, especially since the humidity and my coaching in the Palembang heat demanded multiple baths each day.

But back to our State Department visitor. Upon meeting her, my host father, General Soebutu, affectionately known as *Pak* in his home, graciously asked Lilly if she wanted to use the bathroom to freshen up before the afternoon tea. After her long trip from Jakarta, she hastily responded, "Wonderful!" She definitely wanted to wash up before she ate. Now, Lilly in no way resembled her namesake, a delicate flower. Western women tend to be much larger than most petite Indonesian ladies, but Lilly was large even for an American woman—heavily endowed from top to bottom!

Well, while Lilly was taking her mandi, the rest of us—my host, his wife, their children, and me—were in the front room waiting for Lilly to emerge from the bathroom. After a while, I became concerned about the inordinate amount of time she was spending taking her mandi. As time wore on, I began to fidget nervously, especially when Lilly's "freshening up" took longer than expected and was accompanied with profanity echoing down the hallway. None of us in the tea room made eye contact, as Lilly's swearing mingled with the sounds of splashing water and the metallic bangs of tub and bucket meeting. My hope was that Pak and his family could not distinguish the muffled foul language. As matters eventually settled down in the bathroom, the last clear complaint could be heard: "Ridiculous! How do you expect anyone to take a bath in here? Whoa! That was a tight fit!"

The only imagery I could conjure up came from the sounds in the bathroom, but when Lilly emerged, her face and limp hair said it all. In horror, we realized that she had polluted our week's bathing water by squeezing her entire body into the small water storage basin—our precious mandi! But at least the resulting laughter from everyone eased the tension and paved the way for a jovial afternoon tea with General Soebutu and his family. It dawned on me that day that I had become so accustomed to living in this wonderful, different land that I had failed to explain to a compatriot something as basic as taking a mandi in Indonesia.

8

Arrested

"Drive carefully, and don't get arrested! Especially you, Burghdorf!" These were the last warning words that Alex Shakow said to us as we finished tuning up our Ducati 55cc motorbikes. Since I had walked the dirt roads and used public transport for six months, I was in awe of my motorbike. It seemed beautifully streamlined, as though it were right out of a Buck Roger's futuristic episode. Besides being handsome in design and color, it was extremely loud for a 50cc bike. The major purpose of the bikes was to help volunteers set up coaching clinics in the rural areas outside major cities in Indonesia. The roads in Palembang, especially during the wet season, were often impassable due to the heavy cargo trucks traversing the roads that caused deep ruts and holes. On one occasion, I remember seeing the top of a truck's cab buried up to its windows in a mud hole. The deterioration of the roads not only affected trucks but small forms of transportation, too, such as motorbikes.

Hitting ruts repeatedly and bouncing in and out of holes like a jackrabbit put tremendous pressure on the bolts and the front fork of my motorbike. Consequently, my front license plate had fallen off unbeknownst to me. When and where it had fallen off, I had no clue.

I had no idea there was even a problem until a diminutive traffic policeman with a large ego came running toward me. He was dressed in his khaki uniform, a white sash crossing his chest, shiny black boots, an officer's hat, and dark glasses, which hid his eyes. As he ran, he waved his *pistola* and shouted *"Berhenti! Berhenti!"* (Stop! Stop!) Needless to say, I came to a sudden halt, with the vanishing confidence of one who thinks he has it all under control but obviously doesn't. As the policeman continued his pursuit, he waved his *pistola* and ordered me to get off the motorbike immediately and step far aside. After a few moments of inspecting the front of the motorbike, he returned with a wicked glee on his face and drew my attention to the front of the motorbike where the license plate should have been. To say the least, I was dumbfounded! In defense of myself, I threw up my hands, saying, *"Hilang! Hilang!"* (Lost! Lost!) and promised to replace it as soon as possible. Looking at his stern, cynical face, however, I knew it would take more than a feeble promise.

His strident, commanding response, "I am going to arrest you and take you to the police station," certainly caught my attention. All I could think was, "Wait until Alex hears about this!" As I protested in disbelief, the policeman repeated his command more vehemently, "You go to jail—now!" Meanwhile, a small crowd of bystanders started to gather on the corner of Sudirman and Iskandar Boulevards, one of the busiest intersections in Palembang. How amusing to watch an Indonesian policeman arrest a young American!

Sensing the growing fickleness of the crowd and the need to exert his authority, the policeman then shouted in a military-type voice, "You get on the back of the motorbike. I will take you to the police station—now!" Hearing this command, the crowd grew more vocal and some started to jeer at the policeman. Feeling it was crucial for me to comply with his commands in order to keep peace and to express my respect for his authority, I nervously and somewhat awkwardly mounted the back rack that could be used for a luggage rack or a child's seat.

Imagine a 225-pound man on the luggage rack, holding on to a small Indonesian policeman weighting no more than 130 pounds! This bizarre scene brought more laughter from the gathering crowd. With so much weight on the back, it was a wonder that the front tire did not lift off the pavement. By this time, some people in the crowd were bent over with laughter, and others were crying hysterically. I even heard some of my students shouting, "Oh, Mr. Paul! Oh, Mr. Paul!"

The crowd's responses continued to vary from laughter to jeers as the policeman tried to synchronize the clutch with the gas lever. Each time, the bike would lunge forward several feet—and then die. After several futile attempts, I quietly suggested that I exchange seats with "Pak," another use of the polite term for a respected elder. He could sit on the luggage rack, and I would drive us to the police station. Pak responded with a firm, *"Tidak!"* (No!)

Again, the little policeman tried to start the bike and again it stalled. Again and again! Each failure to start the motor brought even more jeers and laughter. I anxiously recalled that Peace Corps officials had warned us to avoid escalating crowds that could go *amuk,* the Indonesian term meaning to go into a murderous frenzy or rage. In English, we have adopted the term "going amuck" or "going amok." So, sensing that the tone of the crowd was turning more hostile, I again offered to exchange places with the policeman. Again he refused.

As the hostile mood began to border on being volatile, there came a turning point. Suddenly, acting as if he had a brilliant idea, the policeman turned to me, officiously suggesting that he ride on the luggage rack and that I drive us to the police station. Feigning respectful surprise, I responded, "Ah ha! That's a good idea!" I quickly mounted the front seat as Pak walked slowly, in military stride, to the back of the bike and sat regally on the luggage rack. His haughty carriage immediately brought more jeers and boos than laughter from the unsettled crowd. As this policeman held tightly to my waist, my heart went out to him; his hands were shaking. Thankfully, the bike started with the first kick, and we left the raucous crowd behind in a thundering cloud of dust.

As soon as he sensed he was out of danger, the little policeman reverted back to his old arrogant self by giving directions to the police station as military commands that I had to obey immediately. When we reached the Palembang police precinct, the commanding officer there met us with an incredulous expression on his face as we approached the locked front gate. Hearing the reason for my arrest from the officious policeman, the commanding officer's stern face broke into a smile, which he quickly suppressed. Meanwhile, the other policemen at the headquarters, observing the comic-irony of the situation, managed to maintain their composure and stifle their laughter.

The commanding officer quickly took control of the situation by ordering the gates opened and then demanding that all the police officers, along with me and my motorbike, come to attention. I was quickly escorted down the walkway before all present to face the commanding officer's judgment.

The commanding officer, in an attempt to save face for all and to administer justice, ordered that I be removed immediately and placed into a solitary jail cell until I could replace my license plate. Then meeting me at my cell, he provided me with cardboard and a black crayon for a temporary license, a refreshing drink, and an understanding smile. What a wise diplomat! While I was making the new license, I could hear police officers in the compound talking about the humor of my arrest, especially the comic arrival at the locked gates. Next, the wise commander had the arresting officer accompany me to my motorbike and help me attach the license.

When all was finished, everyone in the compound clapped and cheered as though something heroic had been accomplished. In the presence of all his officers, the commander officially thanked the arresting officer for his vigilance in detecting the missing license plate. This act of kindness on the part of the commander certainly protected the dignity of the arresting officer. Turning to me, he lectured me on the importance of following the laws and maintaining my bike. Before all present, he officially dismissed the charge against me and handed me the keys to my motorbike.

As I left the compound, I noticed the other policemen gathering around the "hero," mimicking his grand motorbike entrance, and bursting into laughter. The rest of the ride home provided me the time to contemplate life lessons about respecting elders, protecting others' dignity, and honoring those in authority, lessons basic to surviving anywhere, including Indonesia.

9

Moon River

Artist: Lies (Last name unknown; drawing from author's personal letters)

L ife's ironies bombarded me daily. In October 1963, I found myself at a formal party, savoring rounds of fancy drinks and mounds of Indonesian delicacies. It was the gala opening of the Pusri Fertilizer Plant, the first to produce urea fertilizer pellets that would revolutionize crop production in Asia, especially throughout Indonesia. The Urea Fertilizer Project, which was started in 1959 and completed 1963, held the promise of multiple-crop production each year, thereby reducing malnutrition, a scourge of mankind throughout history. Unfortunately, even as I write this book, millions of people are suffering from malnutrition worldwide. Ironically, at the gala opening I was feasting with three hundred people dressed in formal attire to celebrate the hope of reducing human suffering.

The Pusri plant started operations on October 16, 1963, with an annual production capacity of one hundred thousand tons of fertilizer. To mark the completion of the project, the night was to be filled with special recognitions, food, and dancing. The evening was designed to honor Indonesia as the host country, the United States for its technological and financial support, and Morrison-Knudsen of Asia for finishing the project ahead of schedule. Security was understandably tight, due to the historical significance of this first chemical fertilizer plant and due to the presence of many dignitaries.

Attendance was by special invitation only. By that time, I had left the Bahar family and moved in with the general, who was a prominent citizen of Palembang. As could be expected, he had received an invitation to the Pusri event. He then asked me to join the celebration with him and his beautiful wife and their four children.

Of course, I accepted the invitation. I also recognized the fine line I lived in Indonesia as a Peace Corps volunteer and also as a representative of the United States. I had become very comfortable and truly happy coaching athletes in the rural villages and interacting with my students and colleagues at the university. However, as a Peace Corps volunteer, doors opened to adventures and formal events that the average Indonesian never experienced. On a humorous note, I must confess to attending an American embassy function where I stole cookies. While some people were occupied with the flowing alcohol, my Peace Corps buddies and I focused on the pastries that we had not seen for many months, possibly a year. When our stomachs were full, we proceeded to fill our coat pockets with cookies. On a serious note, however, I keenly recognized the dichotomy between President Kennedy's vision that we live at the level of the host nationals and the reality of being among the few Americans who were invited to elite social functions. I walked a fine line.

And so I joined my host family and the many dignitaries who had been invited to the Pusri celebration. Since President Sukarno was in Bandung, Java, on important government business, his daughter, Miss Megawati, represented him and Indonesia at the celebration. Megawati was Sukarno's second child and the first daughter of Fatmawati, one of Sukarno's nine wives. Megawati, although young, had represented her father and country on other diplomatic missions. In fact, she already was becoming a favorite among the populace. Prominent members of President Sukarno's cabinet, along with members of the American diplomatic corps, were present. And, of course, the celebration included prominent Palembang citizens, such as my host father and his wife, known to me as Pak and Ibu. The president's elite police and the Palembang mobile police were at the gala night to ensure safety for everyone. This was a *big* occasion.

The Indonesian delegation had gathered together in a small group across the dance floor from where I was standing with Pak, who was happily guarding the "punch bowl" with an occasional lapse of abstinence. Pusri's banquet hall easily held the three hundred guests. Tables beautifully decorated with batik tablecloths lined all sides of the dance floor so that people could eat and socialize during the evening's events.

It was a magical night, and excitement permeated the evening air. People started to congregate in front of the podium when a well-dressed official from Morrison-Knudsen approached the microphone. The people in the hall, sensing that something was about to happen, became quiet. The local band, The Sumatran Nights, brought their music to an end. The master of ceremonies welcomed everyone and then proceeded to provide a brief history of the Pusri Project.

While the emcee was talking, my eyes drifted across the dance floor to a beautiful young lady among the Indonesian delegation. From where I stood, it seemed people were going out of their way to honor her with introductions and polite bows and by serving her food and drink. Even President Sukarno's elite guards seemed to have an interest in her.

The emcee opened the official ceremony by saying, "Tonight we celebrate an important milestone in Indonesia's industrial progress as well as in its war on malnutrition. It is my honor to ask the director of Morrison-Knudsen Asia to come forward. And representing Indonesia and President Sukarno, I would like to invite his daughter, Miss Megawati, to join us." So that was she! The attractive woman who had caught my eye just minutes before. The guests applauded as the director and Miss Megawati started down the center aisle to the podium. It was evident that this was a proud moment for Morrison-Knudsen, as the emcee reiterated the company's success in completing the fertilizer plant ahead of schedule. Miss Megawati graciously thanked everyone on behalf of her father and the Indonesian people. Commemorative plaques and symbolic golden keys to the Pusri plant were presented, as thunderous applause erupted throughout the hall. My unbelieving eyes followed Miss Megawati as she then returned to her delegation.

The band started to play a variety of songs from the forties, fifties, and early sixties. Favorite Glen Miller tunes brought folks to the dance floor. "Peggy Sue" and "Sherry" got people hopping. And, of course, songs from Elvis Presley, the Platters, and the Beatles struck a lively chord with the younger crowd, even in Indonesia.

At the sound of the music, waiters dressed in traditional Indonesian garb started serving food: *nasi goreng* (fried rice), *ikan goreng* (fried fish), *pais udang* (prawn pieces), and *daging manis* (sweet beef), followed by dessert and coffee. A special cake, decorated in the colors of the Indonesian flag, added to the festivities.

After all the tables had been served, the emcee announced the first dance. The Sumatran Nights played a variety of music that both the young and old enjoyed. A few more songs and dances went by before an important Indonesian official approached me, asking if I would like to dance with Miss Megawati, who was again standing among the Indonesian elite across the dance floor. Of course, I responded with a prompt, "Yes. I would be honored."

Inside, however, my nerves took over. It didn't help when Pak, my Indonesian father, leaned over and said to me, *"Hati! Hati!"* (Careful! Careful!) in a slurred voice. "Paul," he then added, "don't step on her feet!" With Pak's words ringing in my ears, I walked self-consciously across the dance floor to meet her. I had enough time to recall instructors at Peace Corps training warning, "Do not step on people's feet; it's highly offensive. In Ambon Province, the insult of walking on another's feet can result in a fight and even death." Grateful for an opportunity to harness my shyness as the Indonesian officer accompanied me across the dance floor, I approached the president's daughter, who happened to be smiling at me. I was formally introduced to Miss Megawati, and reeling somewhat from the reality of who she was, I gathered enough of my wits to strike up a conversation. Surrounded by her entourage, we quietly shared some small talk before the emcee called for the next dance.

She cordially extended her right hand to me as we walked slowly to the center of the floor. I could feel hundreds of eyes (especially from the president's special police) watching my every step. As the band played "Moon River," I gently, oh so gently, put my arm around her waist and led her through the dance without once stepping on her delicate feet! We had fun simply enjoying the music and the moment. She danced beautifully;

her experience dancing at other formal occasions certainly made me look good too! Initially Megawati and I talked about small stuff.

And then I asked, "What is it like to be the president's daughter?" She looked at me earnestly with her large, almond-shaped eyes and tactfully replied, "What I enjoy most about representing my father, President Sukarno, is meeting people from all over the world, like meeting you tonight." Her English was excellent, just as one would expect from someone like her, who was educated at Bandung University and at the University of Jakarta. When I told her I was teaching English at the University of Sriwidjaja, she became shy. She shouldn't have.

With her ability to make people feel at ease, the time dancing with her was actually fun and flew by quickly. What probably should have been one dance turned out to be more. What could have been an awkward time turned out to be a happy lifetime memory. After we danced a last dance to "Red Sails in the Sunset," I escorted her to the other side of the dance floor, where her entourage awaited her. As I thanked her for the dances, I realized that it had been a wonderful, innocent time of enjoying each other's company—nothing more than East meeting West. She gave me her hand again and simply said, "Thank you, Paul," with a radiant smile that I will never forget. Then with a squeeze to my arm and with that unforgettable smile, she returned to her friends.

The Sumatran Nights played "Moon River" again as people prepared to leave. Pak, too, was attempting to gather his wits and depart, but he could not even get out of his seat without stumbling. His speech was slurred and his eyes glazed. When he collided with his wife, knocking over her coffee, it became clear to my "family" and to those around us that Pak was drunk. He certainly was in no condition to drive us home in his jeep, but how does a twenty-three-year-old young man tell a famous, retired seventy-year-old general that he is too drunk to drive? His timid wife, his children, and his friends pleaded with him not to drive. "I'm just fine! I can drive home. I'm fine!" was his commanding, slurred response. He would not relent. Climbing into the driver's seat and waiting for the presidential motorcade to pass, however, Pak soon fell asleep at the driver's wheel. Ibu, in an attempt to save face, gently awakened him and asked, "General, since you are so tired, would you like Paul to drive us all home?"

"Yes," he responded groggily, "but first I want to show him how to operate my jeep. And I'll sit up front to navigate the trip home." Several officers and I rushed to assist tipsy Pak around the front of the jeep to the passenger's side where he could still be the commander of the trip home!

I then quickly jumped into the driver's seat and started to acquaint myself with the controls. As I sat there with Pak in the front passenger seat and Ibu and the four children huddling together on the back bench, the official military police motorcade revved their motors to indicate the departure of the dignitaries. I noticed in my rearview mirror a polished black limousine with presidential plates and Indonesian flags mounted on the front fenders approaching to depart through the gates of the Pusri compound. Suddenly, the limousine came alongside our waiting vehicle. For a flash—just a moment in time—Miss Megawati's radiant smile met my gaze. Then, with a simple wave of her hand, she mouthed, "Goodbye." Years later, that same charm and gracious smile would help to win the hearts of her people, and she would become the first female president of Indonesia.

10

The Christmas Gift

Finally, winter break arrived after an enjoyable and challenging semester teaching English literature at the University of Sriwidjaja. With more time on my hands and Christmas just a few days away, a full-blown case of homesickness set in. Feeling sorry for myself, I lounged next to the window, watching the monsoon rain fall while I listened to "I'm Dreaming of a White Christmas," by Bing Crosby, for the tenth time (well, maybe only the fifth time). My spirits continued falling with the incessant rain.

Christmas in Indonesia contrasted painfully with Christmas at home. Instead of a decorated Christmas tree infusing my room with fresh pine scents, rugged palm trees whipped and screamed wildly in the wind. Instead of colorful Christmas lights blinking off and on to spread holiday cheer, there was the one essential bare light bulb glaring from the ceiling. And instead of a fresh blanket of snow on the ground, there were hopeless, rut-filled muddy roads. Oh, how I hurt!

Although the fall semester had ended well, there was the usual letdown associated with a period of intense work. Unfortunately, more Peace Corps volunteers quit due to homesickness before finishing their two years than any other factor. Perhaps the best prevention for loneliness overseas is a purposeful job or a responsibility that keeps one accountable daily and one that results in a sense of accomplishment and well-being. Of course, that is true anywhere, for anyone. However, Peace Corps volunteers without clearly defined jobs, followed by encroaching discouragement, do not even have their culture, language, or social systems to turn to for support. Area directors are key to laying the groundwork for definite jobs and housing before the volunteers arrive. Yes, I had initially been disappointed that Palembang was not ready to use my skills, but we volunteers also have opportunities for growth as we work patiently within new systems and advocate for ourselves.

The first step out of my quagmire came when I took the initiative to find a job—on my own. I also managed to form new relationships when I volunteered to lead an English conversation class for women. Of course, the class drew educated and prominent women who had the luxury of time and means to attend. It was one of the women in that class who encouraged me to apply for a teaching position at the University of Sriwidjaja.

And, yes, I had reached out during my first difficult weeks at Hotel Swarma Dwipa by making contact with Bob and Pat Gonia, missionaries working in Palembang. Their continuing friendship, open hearts, and dinner invitations for those initial six months had done much to ease my loneliness and to support my transition. However, on that rainy afternoon, with the Christmas music playing, I continued dreaming of home. Ironically, these were not the dreams of abundant gifts and traditional delicious food but of meaningful times with my own family, such as when we worked with orphans who lived on top of a landfill outside the city limits of Ensenada, Mexico.

My reality, nevertheless, was Palembang at Christmas. Several weeks prior, when I had been sharing with Bob Gonia about my homesickness, we both agreed that it was difficult handling the ache of being away from family and friends during the holidays. He recalled his childhood in Tennessee, living in poverty but also in a family that clung happily to traditions and laughter. My California roots included extended family gatherings at Uncle Truman's Malibu beach home, where cousins romped in the winter sun and musical aunties tried to herd us around the piano for Christmas songs of the faith. Bob and I were on the same page as we both longed for Christmas treasures found much deeper than in toys and trinkets.

My reality still was Christmas in Palembang. With thoughts of loneliness running through my mind and the tropical rain lashing upon the window of my room, I was trying to prepare for the next semester's class by organizing my lecture notes on *Gulliver's Travels,* by Jonathan Swift.

Unexpectedly, I glanced outside to see Bob Gonia's green pickup truck pull into my muddy driveway. Did he have letters from home? Was he inviting me to a holiday party? Or did he carry bad news about his two-year-old son, who had recently been diagnosed with terminal liver cancer? Fearing the worst, I opened the door with uncertainty. The first words out of Bob's mouth began a life-changing journey for me: "Hey Paul, I have a Christmas gift for you, but you need to take a long ride into the jungle with me to receive it." I couldn't believe that Bob and Pat would be thinking of me at this season, when they were struggling with a hopeless diagnosis for their son. However, I was soon to experience that Bob was a unique human who would put the needs of others before his own.

As I rushed into the bedroom to get my backpack, Bob yelled from the sitting room, "Take some good walking shoes and a light jacket. We may not be back before dark."

"Bob, where are we going?" I asked.

"You'll soon see. Get in!" was his only response.

As I peeked into the bed of the truck, I spied several large cardboard boxes unwrapped and unmarked. Honestly, there wasn't anything that might resemble a Christmas gift for me.

Bob turned down the road toward the Palembang airport, but then veered onto a well-traveled road to the Musi River. Since the truck was four-wheel drive and raised, most roads presented no problems in the wet season. After about one hour of driving, we came to a landing for the Shell-Stanvac oil refinery. Since there was only one ferry, we both got out of the truck and waited for the ferry to return from the other side. The putrid Musi River, still filled with trash and the occasional carcasses of dead animals, continued its journey to the ocean, leaving its brown scum on the riverbanks where people still washed clothes, brushed their teeth, collected drinking water, and even defecated! "This country needs clean, potable water," moaned Bob.

I agreed as I thought to myself, "Coaches train athletes to perform spectacularly on the world stages, but what Indonesia really needs is health and water management experts."

Turning our backs to the river, we also talked about our personal concerns, including homesickness. As Bob described the physical and psychological effects of homesickness on its victims, I shook my head in affirmation. It was comforting to know that Bob understood what I was experiencing. He then quietly shared with me how difficult it was for him and Pat to be away from home, separated from their families at this time when his son was battling liver cancer. Deep inside, I sensed that my pain paled in comparison to the suffering of those on the riverbank and of the man standing beside me. Suddenly I felt selfish as I wiped tears from my eyes and asked Bob to forgive my self-centeredness. Putting his arm around my shoulder, he said, "Paul, we need to pray for God's strength to keep us strong in this needy country and through the difficult times that lie ahead. For you, Paul, I pray that you will be able to face and overcome your homesickness in order to be effective here, and for me to be able to face my son's impending death without being bitter."

With the arrival of the rickety ferry, Bob revved the truck engine in order to make it up the gangplank and onto the ferry for the trip across the Musi. As Bob parked his truck on board in a designated space, I still didn't know where he was taking me. The ferry slowly made its way across the Musi while Bob and I continued talking about Christmas. As we held onto the wooden siding while the ferry puttered slowly across the river, Bob quietly asked, "Paul, since you are an English major, I wonder if you ever read the short story "The Gift of the Magi"?

"Yes. You mean the story of Jim and Della, two newlyweds who sacrifice their greatest treasures in order to buy gifts for each other."

"Well, Paul, isn't that what Christmas is really about?"

I easily agreed it wasn't just the gifts, but I continued to dwell on my loneliness. Finally, Bob looked me straight in the eyes and cut me short, saying, "Paul, *it is not all about you!*" With Bob's forthright statement, punctuated by the *boom!* of the ferry reaching the dock, we quickly returned to the truck to disembark.

We must have driven another hour on a dirt road through dense jungle when suddenly we came to a well-manicured area with conical white stick houses built neatly in a semi-circle facing the road. Stopping the truck near the main building, Bob asked me to help him carry the boxes to the commons room used for storage, group gatherings, and a dining room. Bob then quietly said to me, "Paul, this is a sanatorium for the treatment of leprosy." I asked about leprosy since all I knew was that it was an "untouchables" disease mentioned in ancient times. Bob explained, "It is a disfiguring disease that usually affects the skin and peripheral nerves. Paul, the affected people often lose their fingers, toes, and facial features due to nerve damage."

"So, Bob, is that why they have a leper colony way out here, to isolate these people from healthy humans?"

"Don't worry! The disease is not contagious, even though they have been shunned throughout history."

"I thought Bob said he had a Christmas gift for me," I quipped to myself. "Surely this is not it!"

Bob and I walked over to the first conical house and knocked on the wooden door. The first person who came to the door was a feeble man with no nose or mouth, just a gaping hole as large as my fist. Taken aback at the sight of his face, my eyes moved quickly down to his feet. Where his feet should have been, there were two ulcerated stubs with toes missing. As he spoke, my eyes rose to meet his, and I discovered a beautiful smile in his eyes. And to think that I was down in the dumps about being homesick! The next person who greeted us came crawling to the door because she was missing both of her feet up to her scarred, swollen ankles, yet her beautiful, radiant face belied her physical condition. In Bahasa Indonesian, she welcomed us with: *"Selamat Hari Natal"* (Merry Christmas). The last person who came to the door was a younger man who also had no feet. These three lepers welcomed us proudly into their whitewashed house. Even though these people lived with a devastating disease, their house was simple, organized, and welcoming. The dirt floors were clean and newly swept, the sweep marks still in the dirt. There were no pungent odors of decaying flesh that might cause a visitor to withdraw. Bob did most of the talking, in Bahasa Indonesian, as we sat around on wooden boxes.

To my surprise, these people were joyous and went out of their way to make us feel welcomed. In fact, a family atmosphere permeated the room. Neither Bob nor I felt uncomfortable, just thankful that we could spend a little time with them at Christmas. Actually, I felt honored to be their guest. What fun it was to surprise them as we pulled the boxes off the truck and revealed clothes and canned food to their shouts of joy! They, in turn, responded with small handcrafted gifts, their eyes shining with the radiance of those who truly give.

As I listened to their merry talk and laughter, I realized the life-gift that they had given me. They had few physical reasons to be happy, and I had everything physical to be happy about, yet I was miserable in my own self-absorption. Bob's words kept running through my mind: *"Paul, it isn't all about you."* And to this he later added, "I wanted you to realize the wonderful gifts God has already bestowed upon you. This is why I brought you here, to experience the genuine joy that these people possess, even in light of their physical conditions and poverty. It is the inner joy that only God can give when they know they are loved unconditionally and as they love others without reservation. Now it is time for you to make your own personal life response. Merry Christmas, Paul."

Even today, fifty years later, that afternoon with the lepers was the best Christmas gift I have ever received. Yes, it was a gift that has lasted a lifetime. Thank you, Bob, for helping me to look past myself, to realize it is not all about me.

IOWA-INDONESIA PEACE CORPS VOLUNTEERS

February 22 – May 17, 1963

Row 1: Ed Axline, Jan Axline, Paul Burghdorf, Bob Dakan, Dick Doughty
Row 2: Vic Godfrey, Ron Haedt, Ken Hollis, Rich Kravitz, George Larson
Row 3: Norm Majors, Jim Morrisey, Peter Morrissey, Dan Mouton, Jim Noonan
Row 4: Nancy Rickert, Jordan Safine, John Second, Peter Weng

**Peace Corps Training – Graduation Picture
at University of Iowa, May 17, 1963**

Meeting President John F. Kennedy in the Rose Garden May 17, 1963

Meeting President John F. Kennedy May 17, 1963

Playing softball with Sargeant Shriver May 17, 1963

Arrival in Jakarta, June 1, 1963

Meeting Madame Hartini June 2, 1963

The Grand Room in Madame Hartini's Palace June 2, 1963

Coaching Volleyball – University of Sriwidjaja students

Teaching volleyball skills

Sad Wedding Couple

Formal wedding picture of student from university class

University Students, 1964 class

Friends in Palembang

11

The Governor's Beautiful Wife

In the tropics, there are two seasons, the wet and the dry. May announces the coming of the dry season, with its hot, humid weather accompanied by the end of another school year and the beginning of social gatherings to welcome the drier, more carefree days. It was during this time of year that the governor of South Sumatra would hold his annual lawn party on the lavish grounds of his mansion. Prominent people from all over South Sumatra were invited. Among those honored with an invitation were governors from other Indonesian provinces, high-ranking military officers, police magistrates, personnel from foreign embassies, and dignitaries from the Palembang community. Everyone in Palembang longed to attend the prestigious party due to its reputation for celebrity entertainment and delicious South Sumatran cuisine. The governor's party was traditionally held on June 16, Palembang's historical birthday. With the celebration fast approaching, the governor and his staff finalized the list of guests and sent out the coveted invitations. The upcoming party was the talk of the town, with people speculating about the guest list, dreaming about personal invitations, imagining the lavish food, and predicting the entertainment. Since Balinese culture fascinated the governor's wife, gamelan music and traditional Balinese dancing might highlight the year's event. Rumors were rampant and anticipation was high.

In addition to teaching English at the University of Sriwidjaja, I continued to conduct several English conversation classes that included prominent women of the area. For several weeks, I was privy to the women's lively conversations about the upcoming governor's party. Did I ever learn about social networking! Yes, even in Palembang! As I was returning home one afternoon, I recalled their social "twitter" and could understand anew the excitement surrounding a royal event. Perhaps one of my students would be the fortunate person to receive an invitation.

So, as I entered my bedroom and approached my desk, I was shocked to discover that I, indeed, had received a hand-delivered, prized invitation to the governor's lawn party. I really had no idea that I would be invited to such an elite social gathering. After all, who was I in Palembang society? But there it was, the invitation with my name on it. My ego allowed me to believe momentarily that it was because of my fine teaching at the university or that it was because I had achieved diplomatic success as a Peace Corps volunteer. I dreamed that my attendance at the party would help to further American diplomacy, perhaps even to lessen the animosity between Indonesia and the United States. And the glory could be all mine!

In a country where social position speaks loudly, I was certainly among the least of the socially elite guests. To my surprise upon arrival at the party, the official host seated me in the garden just across from the governor's wife. Her strikingly beautiful face belied her unusual body. She was not quite five feet tall, which accounted for the fact that when she was seated, her small shoes did not reach the lawn. Even though she was rather short, she must have been at least five or more feet in circumference! A large wife in Indonesian culture is a barometer of her husband's wealth, and this governor's wife was definitely a living symbol of his affluence. This particular balmy evening, she was wearing a sarong with a beautiful blue blouse. As I distinctly recall, the blouse was a see-through kind with elaborate white designs embossed on a rich blue background. I must point out that occasionally I caught her looking down at the front of her dazzling blouse with a sense of satisfaction and pride. After all, her blouse appeared to be new, and it was probably the only one of its kind in Palembang. Even though she was quite short, the blouse proudly displayed her large breasts. In an attempt to strike up conversation with her, I introduced myself. As I did, I caught her eyes roaming to more socially prominent guests with whom she could engage in conversation. The new chief of police and his wife were six seats down from her. The rektor of the University of Sriwidjaja was seated two rows behind her.

Our short conversation was interrupted by the official introduction of her husband, the governor, who was wearing a traditional Indonesian white sultan shirt, dark slacks, and a merdeka independence hat. After the governor was introduced with much pomp and circumstance, waiters dressed in brown batik shirts and black trousers served delicious hors d'oeuvres of frog legs, shrimp, and tropical drinks, while the band played music from the fifties and sixties. Later, exotic Indonesian music would provide the background for the dinner.

For the main course, servers fanned into the crowd with the traditional rice dish of nasi goreng, a generous helping of stir-fried spicy rice topped with meat. (As was often the case, I did not recognize the specific kind of meat so simply categorized it in my mind as "mystery meat.") My helping of meat seemed to be balanced precariously on top of a mountain of steaming, fragrant rice.

Each guest received a fork and a large spoon made of Bangka tin with which to cut the meat. The trick was to hold down the meat with the fork and then to dexterously use the edge of the spoon in the other hand to cut the meat into bite-sized portions while attempting to balance the bowl of rice on one's knees. The spoon served as a knife in Indonesian cutlery.

At the same time, I was trying to engage the governor's wife in small talk. After several attempts to slice the meat with the edge of the spoon, I noticed the governor's wife looking, with raised eyebrows, impatiently across at me. With her shrill voice of encouragement, she barked, *"Makan! Makan!"* (Eat! Eat!). Her little legs would move up and down like pistons with every pronouncement, never once touching the ground. I knew I had to cut the meat and start eating it quickly. My Indonesian cultural instructor had stressed the importance of waiting until the hostess invites guests to eat, and he had said that not liking the food would be an insult. At that point in the dinner, it seemed to me that time was of the essence. In desperation to cut the meat, I again tried but was unable even to graze its surface, not even with several small cuts.

With the governor's wife's command of *"Makan! Makan!"* pounding in my ears, I decided to put forth my best effort into cutting the meat. So with renewed strength and confidence, I held the fork tightly in one hand and the spoon in the other, as though they were medieval weapons. The call of battle had sounded, and I was now ready. No "mystery meat" would get the best of me! I held my breath, plunged the fork deep into the meat, and powerfully forced the edge of the spoon into the meat. With no fanfare or trumpets of a classic battle, the edge of the spoon again met tough resistance from the meat. But this time, the spoon broke in half.

The downward force caused the spoon to break, shooting the bowl of rice straight across the aisle in the direction of the governor's wife. It seemed like a slow motion movie as I watched the nasi goreng and meat quickly pancake upside down, landing just above her exquisite low-cut blouse!

Her shocked cry and change in appearance brought the servants and the palace guards quickly to her rescue. In the interim, I sat in the chair in a state of shock. When I came to my senses, I took out my handkerchief and leaned over to the governor's wife in an attempt to help clean off the rice. I didn't even know where to begin to help. The bowl of rice had landed upside down just above her breasts, and the nasi goreng and meat in the bowl were sliding down her blouse onto her sarong. At this point, what is a man expected to do to help a woman in distress? My Peace Corps training in cold Iowa had not prepared me adequately.

I politely said my goodbyes to the people around me and proceeded to the governor's platform to offer my official farewell. I was told the governor was not available due to a pressing emergency concerning his wife. I asked the deputy governor to extend my appreciation for the "wonderful" evening before I quickly sought the nearest exit from the garden. As I left the garden with my head down and my pride even lower, I heard one servant say, "Thank you for coming." I painfully thought to myself, "So much for American diplomacy!"

12

Wedding Blues

**Artist: Lies (Last name unknown; drawing
from author's personal letters)**

Sri could have been featured as the bride of the month in *Modern Bride* magazine. In addition to her natural beauty and radiant smile, her personality attracted others to her. Especially in my university class, her vibrant personality lifted spirits when academic work was too weighty. Like a fresh breeze in a stuffy room, she could provide the welcomed lift. So why was she so unhappy? She had become more and more miserable as her wedding day approached. Her beautiful face, in fact, was puffy on her wedding day because of her incessant weeping. Why all the crying before such a special occasion?

In Indonesian Muslim weddings, the celebrations would usually last seven days. Often on the seventh day, the entire village was invited to join in the celebrations. Everyone would feast on lavish Indonesian cuisine and enjoy a band playing popular music, the traditional contrasted with the contemporary.

Since Sri was one of my English literature students at the University of Sriwidjaja, I was privileged to be among the guests invited to celebrate on the seventh day of the wedding. Immediately upon my arrival, I noticed Sri's serious expression and swollen face, even though it was covered with makeup, and she was dressed in sparkling traditional wedding attire. From her head to feet, she was exquisite. Her expressionless face, however, revealed another story. I continued to wonder why she had been crying.

According to tradition, I joined the guests on the customary tour of the bride's house. The highlight was the bride's bedroom, which was decorated with lace curtains that served as a canopy for the bed. An opulent bedspread was decorated with embroidered flowers, and fresh flower pedals provided scents that permeated the bridal room. The bride was sitting on the bed dressed in her flowered, silk wedding dress and an ornate silver headdress, highlighted by dangling sliver beads. Beside her stood the groom, dressed proudly in his family's traditional silk robes. His head was also crowned with an elaborately crafted silver covering. Neither was smiling. My photo album still has the photo of a beautifully adorned Indonesian young woman sitting next to her husband, with a blank stare masking her emotions. Of course, I assumed that it was my American perspective that interpreted their expressions as sad, but even Sri's friends pointed out that she seemed withdrawn and extremely unhappy. What a contrast to the joyful young lady I remembered from class.

After the tour of the bedroom, guests were directed to two separate large rooms. The women were happily and noisily chattering among themselves in one room. In the other sat the men talking and probably awaiting the food. With the exotic, spicy aromas permeating the house, I certainly kept my eye on the hallway leading from the cooking area. I joined the men sitting cross-legged on the floor. Some of these men knew Sri from university classes, and others were friends of the family or guests from the village. Perhaps not as lively as the women's chatter, the men's laughter reflected a jovial brotherhood as they endured the wedding formalities, shared jokes, and anticipated the feast.

I overheard several men talking matter-of-factly about Sri's sadness due to the fact that this was an arranged marriage. The university friends were concerned because Sri had not met her husband before the day of the wedding. He was fifty years old. She was twenty-five. But he was wealthy! My gnawing questions had been answered, and I understood why Sri appeared so solemn but her parents were smiling with pleasure. I was surprised that some of Sri's friends thought they were cheering her up by saying, "At least you have married a wealthy man, one that can take care of all your needs."

Cultural differences certainly existed, and I had much to learn. Like so many young American adventurers, I could not expect everyone to see from my American perspective. Yes, Sri was an intelligent, capable university woman. Yes, her family demanded an arranged marriage. And, yes, I continued to struggle with cultural differences, not always coming up with easy, quick answers to complicated issues.

While I was seated on the floor with the men, servers began to offer appetizers. In a land where some people have barely enough to eat, I was surprised at the abundance of food. It must have taken days for the cooks to prepare the wedding feast. The first appetizer, served on a silver tray, was a small cracker topped with fresh shrimp. Delicious! In fact, I had several crackers before the tray was passed on. Trays of delicacies continued. The food was so plentiful that after a while I decided to give my stomach a rest.

The men further down the carpet from where I sat seemed to be having an enjoyable time, periodically laughing heartily with one another. At one point, their excitement seemed to be spreading toward me, like the burning fuse of a firecracker. Thinking that it was no more than friends enjoying the occasion, I looked up to see several men with curious smirks on their faces urging me to try one last appetizer offered from another silver tray. "I bet this one has a kick to it, probably the hot and spicy *sambal* that I love. I'll show them that I can match the best of them when it comes to hot sauces," I thought, as I reached for one of the round-shaped appetizers covered with shredded coconut. The white delicacies contrasted with the decorative banana leaves that held the balls in place. "Mr. Paul, *mencoba. Mencoba*" (Try. Try.), urged the server, with a proud smile on his face.

The first taste was the sweet coconut. Then just as I was expecting to bite into a crisp, hot chili, a man sitting next to me excitedly exclaimed,

"Oh, Mr. Paul, you like fish eyes, too!" Instead of my teeth meeting the chili, my teeth broke through the tough gristle of the fish eye into a liquid inner core. Immediately, my instincts yelled for me to expel the coconut-covered eye, just as my stomach wanted to join forces to vomit the "delicacy" from my heaving mouth. Tears rolled down my cheeks, and my face turned red as I fought a desperate battle to divert an impending social faux pas at dear Sri's wedding. "Oh no! Not another social blunder to haunt me!" I thought, as the fish eye sat precariously lodged somewhere between my mouth and my stomach. My quick eyes revealed no place to hide, no place to spit the fish eye out, and no bushes for escape. After much prodding from my fellow men, however, I managed to swallow the wedding delicacy.

As I sank into the background, I quietly calmed myself, thankful that I had not caused an embarrassing scene as I did at the governor's garden party. Rationalizing to myself, I thought, "Burghdorf, at least you provided some comic relief for the wedding blues." The guests seemed to enjoy the celebrations of the evening. We continued to dine to gamelan music and dance to pop songs played by a live band. Happy conversation and laughter filled the night air, all part of a wedding day in Indonesia. I never saw Sri smile the entire night, except when I was saying my farewells. With a modest grin, she quietly said, "Mr. Paul, I understand that you like fish eyes."

13

The Crazy Betjak Ride

**Artist: Victoria Newell, student at Bandung Alliance
International School, Bandung, Indonesia**

ifty years ago, betjaks were a major form of transportation throughout Indonesia. These three-wheel bicycles, also known as *rickshaws* elsewhere in Asia, come in other versions found in India, where the driver sits at the front of the bike, and in the Philippines, with the driver at the side. Unlike these two versions, the Indonesian betjak has the driver sitting at the rear. Today, betjaks have been banned from the main traffic streets of some large Indonesian cities, such as Jakarta. However, in Bandung, the country's second largest city, some of these unique people-movers still dominate the small, out-of-the-way streets. And they certainly were a part of living there as a Peace Corps volunteer in the 1960s.

Jim, who had been my Peace Corps roommate through the most difficult times of our lives in Indonesia, was leaving for Medan, Sumatra, to coach in a successful competitive track and field program. To be honest, I had some ambivalent feelings about Jim's departure. Medan offered a sports program that would utilize Jim's experience and coaching skills, while the Palembang sports ministry still had provided us very little help in the way of support, not to mention the actual coaching jobs that government officials had offered when they initially assigned Peace Corps volunteers to the various cities. Still, I would miss Jim as a colleague and even more as a loyal friend. Adversity and loneliness had taught us to care for and support each other.

The week before Jim's departure, we entertained Mark, an eccentric house guest from Malaysia. Mark had just completed his two-year commitment as a Peace Corps volunteer and was traveling throughout Indonesia before he headed back to the States. Later, we learned that while serving in Malaysia, Mark had a rather dubious reputation for various reasons. He seemed to have a bent for getting into trouble. He also had a difficult time controlling his alcohol. Often, his drunkenness would accentuate his already eccentric behavior, resulting in impromptu actions.

Little did Jim and I know of Mark's reputation when we decided to take Mark along with us to Palembang's fine restaurant, the Rumah Makan Sriwidjaja, to celebrate Jim's departure. For this occasion, we had saved carefully from our monthly three-dollar pay and from occasional gifts from home. This unique restaurant was situated on a small hill on the outskirts of Palembang, surrounded by flatlands that led down to the mighty Musi River. Since the restaurant was located approximately six kilometers outside of town and up a hill, we decided to take a taxi for this special occasion.

Rumah Maken Sriwidjaja was known for its distinctive South Sumatran cuisine. One of its many specialties was a white fish served with spicy durian sauce accompanied with a spicy, clear soup. My favorite delicacy was succulent frog legs served on nasi goreng.

The inside of the Rumah Maken Sriwidjaja was beautifully decorated with dark teak wood tables and colorful batik wall tapestries surrounding an indoor coy pond. Wide doors led to an expansive patio that encircled the restaurant and offered spectacular views of tropical sunsets with the Musi in the foreground. The Musi River divided Palembang and offered a point of reference as the lights of the city announced the end of the day in a bustling port city. Since it was a warm, humid evening, we settled for a table on the patio. The location of our dinner table allowed us to talk freely without the worry of anyone scrutinizing us.

For some of the time, Jim and I reminisced about our "trial by fire" at the Hotel Swarma Dwipa, which included long, lonely days of homesickness interrupted by our two-meter dashes for the toilet during frequent bouts of dysentery. We had survived and were determined to finish our two-year commitment, a pledge to Indonesia, to the United States, and to ourselves!

Occasionally, between his drinks, Mark would volunteer snippets of his experiences in Malaysia, two years full of adventures and memories to take home. Mark explained that he saw monkeys used in Malaysia to gather coconuts from high perches in the palm trees. They scaled up the tree, picked the coconuts, and then threw them down to the master below, who would put them into gunny sacks. One day, while Mark was standing nearby to watch a monkey at work, he started making faces, sticking his tongue out, and making monkey noises at the busy little worker up in the tree. Before long, the monkey became mad and started throwing the coconuts at Mark. Mark enjoyed the give and take until the upset monkey, like a bolt of lightning from nowhere, charged straight down the tree for Mark, who took off running. Mark was no track star and the monkey outran him. Just as Mark thought he was the loser, the charging monkey came to the end of his tether. Mark took a deep breath and admitted, "I was really scared when that monkey went into attack mode."

Of course, we talked about snakes that night. As Mark was telling about eating cobra at a restaurant in Malaysia, Jim responded, "Yeah, I bet it tasted like chicken. That's what everyone says about all 'mystery meat' that we eat here. Hey, Paul, tell Mark what happened when we were unpacking our bicycles from Singapore."

Before we had the luxury of motorbikes, the Peace Corps purchased bicycles for us to use around Palembang. The bicycles arrived wrapped in sturdy packing crates. Inside the crates, bamboo padding secured the bicycles. Since we had only one set of tools, Jim took his bicycle out first and assembled it, with the bamboo lying in the open carport. Wanting to test the bike, Jim took off for a quick ride around the neighborhood. He returned, saying, "Hey, Paul, look what I found." Coiled on the chain guard was a small green snake with its head raised, flicking its tongue at Jim's leg. It was small and cute, almost like a child's rubber toy snake.

"Hey, little guy," I teased, as I picked up a bamboo stick to play with him. When I knocked him off the bike, he quickly slithered under the nearby bamboo wrapping. Each time I lifted more bamboo, he would dart for a new cover. He even went between my legs once. Three or four times he managed to escape me. The game continued until a house worker approached and spotted our new little friend.

"Bahaja! Bahaja!" (Dangerous! Dangerous!) screamed the young lady. "It thirty-step snake!" Even in her horror, she managed enough English to tell us that once bitten by this extremely poisonous snake, the victim manages to walk only about thirty steps before dying. Jim and I provided quite a spectacle as we jumped straight up, with Jim landing in my arms for the great escape out of the carport. To Mark's next question, "What happened to your little friend?" I replied, "The petite house worker took care of him. She made sure he would never return."

Laughter and exclamations filled our conversation that night. The camaraderie was invigorating, especially when we all three seriously agreed that the highlight of our time in Southeast Asia was in relating to the people, like the Barhars, in our day-to-day life and work.

As the evening progressed, I noticed Mark was talking less and drinking more. Mark's speech began to take on a noticeable slur. In fact, it became difficult to understand him, and it wasn't his Bostonian accent, either. His flushed face eventually took on a sickly green hue, the color of the tapestry on the wall behind him.

Eventually, the waiter kindly informed us that the restaurant would be closing in a half hour and asked if there was anything more that we wanted. Realizing that Mark needed to exit quickly, I asked for the bill, which came to thirty-five hundred rupiahs, more than Jim or I made in a month. Between the two of us, Jim and I were able to pay the bill with a few rupiahs left. There certainly was not enough for a taxi home.

Our only choice was to walk six kilometers or take a betjak home. Fortunately, there were several betjak drivers still waiting for customers, but by the time the three of us finally made it out the front door of the restaurant and down the front steps, there was only one betjak left. Typical of betjak drivers at that time of night, ours was half asleep, curled up on the front seat of his betjak as he awaited customers. Perhaps he planned to sleep there for the night. Arousing him, I offered him twenty rupiahs to take all three of us back to Palembang. At first, he seemed not to understand but then replied, *"Tidak"* (No). He was tired and wanted to sleep outside the restaurant for the night. Gaunt and sinewy like many betjak drivers, he appeared to be sickly.

In desperation, Mark offered the man his leftover food. Jim offered him a small flashlight, and finally I offered him my remaining twenty rupiahs. It must have been Jim's flashlight that sealed the deal as the three of us attempted to squeeze ourselves into the front seat of the betjak. Impossible, especially for three large athletes! The poor betjak driver struggled only a short distance, veering from left to right, when Mark came up with one of his spontaneous ideas. "Hey, guys, I am a cyclist. I can pedal this betjak home." And before we knew what happened, the little betjak driver was seated between Jim and me. Mark was on the bike seat behind us, pedaling away from the restaurant—down the hill.

As we gathered speed, we felt the wind in our faces. The betjak continued gathering speed as it veered from one side of the road to the other. In Mark's reckless abandonment, he ignored the threatening potholes, some large enough to engulf the whole betjak itself. The diminutive driver clung to me, pleading, *"Berhenti! Berhen*ti! (Stop! Stop!) the betjak." Meanwhile, Mark leaned forward shouting, "Speak English, will you! Speak English!" I glanced at Jim, who was usually stoic in threatening situations, only to see real fear in his face. What else could we do but hang on for the wild ride as the betjak careened down the hill out of control.

At this point in our downhill adventure, we realized that Mark could not find the brake for the betjak. His feet fumbled with the pedals, which provided no slowing effect, as the bike continued to gain speed. Where was the brake? Unknown to Mark, it was a lever right between his two legs. But Mark's confusion, inexperience, and fear blinded him. Finally, using the universal language of panicked gestures, the driver pointed to the lever just as we plunged screaming off the road into the darkness of the jungle. The sudden impact caused each of us in the front seat to be ejected through the air into the jungle. Mark had actually flown over the front canopied seat of the betjak and landed in the tropical ferns next to the road. Mark's being drunk had probably saved his life. The remaining three of us were badly bruised, but nothing was broken. The betjak driver had landed safely in the bushes next to Jim and me.

The betjak had plunged off the road and landed upright, with the beautiful art work on the two fenders badly scraped. However, the mechanical parts, including the metal break lever, still worked. The four of us were able to push the betjak out of the roadside ditch onto the road and then to straighten its cloth top. Because the betjak driver probably was renting his betjak and would be held responsible for damages incurred, I made arrangements to pay him the following month for the scratched fender. With a sense of relief and a gratitude for being alive, we said farewell to the betjak driver who delivered us home, this time with Mark seated stolidly in the front seat between Jim and me.

The next day, Jim left for his coaching job in Medan, limping as he boarded the plane. Mark returned to Boston. I returned to the university, thankful to be back to a daily routine with my students, who continued to be my inspiration. And according to the other betjak drivers in the area, our little driver never relinquished his betjak to another American again.

14

Two Bangs That Rocked the World

oping that this was not going to be another harrowing experience flying in a DC-3, I boarded the small Garuda airplane headed for Jakarta for my medical examination before traveling on to the highlands of Bogor for our first in-country Peace Corps conference. I was excited about the opportunity to meet up with my Peace Corps coaching friends after our long first six months in Indonesia. I was not, however, overjoyed about the routine medical examination that required stool and blood samples from everyone.

I was looking forward to some candid discussions about the common challenges affecting the Peace Corps' progress in Indonesia. How were other coaches in our contingent adjusting to this marvelous and varied country? What sports teams were thriving, or at least making good progress? I had some great stories to tell, especially my calamity at the governor's garden party. Who could top my story?

The plane had been in the air for only a few minutes, following the mighty Musi River, when suddenly its twin engines started to sputter, and the plane quickly began losing altitude. This was not a good omen for me, especially considering what I had experienced on previous DC-3 flights.

Right at this tense moment, the pilot banked the plane to the right and made a quick descent back to Palembang Airport. Just before we landed, the pilot's seemingly confident voice came across the intercom system, assuring the passengers that everything was okay and not to worry. Well, at least it was almost okay. The pilot emphasized it was a small "non-mechanical" problem that could be easily corrected once we were back on the ground in Palembang. The pilot asked all passengers to remain seated and calm. He then made an abrupt landing and taxied over to a Shell Oil truck, which was awaiting our return.

Two mechanics dressed in white overalls hurriedly climbed out of the refueling truck. We watched in disbelief as one mechanic climbed onto the right wing, unscrewed the fuel cap to the plane's petrol tank, and began refueling the plane. Twenty minutes later, the mechanic went through the same procedure on the left wing, finally filling what had been empty fuel tanks!

After the mechanics did what they should have done before our original takeoff, they performed a cursory inspection of the entire airplane, as if they were following routine procedures. Only a few of us were able to chuckle as they walked around the little plane and ended the inspection by kicking the plane's tires several times to assure the wide-eyed passengers that all was okay. They apparently wanted us to think all of the activity had been normal maintenance procedures. The mechanics then walked away proudly, acting as if they had saved face in front of the passengers who were still gawking from the plane's window. But we knew the truth!

A few minutes later, the plane started down the runway at full throttle, but this time the two engines purred like satisfied cats rather than old cars sputtering on their last fumes of gasoline.

From the left side of the airplane, I could see that the pilot was again following the Musi River above the dense jungle toward the southern part of Sumatra. Looking out of the windows at the jungle below, I was reminded that the vastness of the Sumatran jungles was second only to the jungles of Kalimantan (also known as Borneo). The jungles below were home to the Sumatran tigers, the black rhinoceros, orangutans, sun bears, and some of the world's biggest and most deadly snakes. I was relieved to know that the plane had fuel, but I was still tempted to worry about its mechanical condition.

After a while, I turned to look for the Sunda Straight. At its narrowest point, the strait stretches only fifteen miles wide between Cape Tua on Sumatra and Cape Puja on Java. It has been an important shipping route for centuries. The Dutch East India Company used the strait as a gateway to Indonesia's Spice Islands when the world developed a passion for the exotic tastes and aromas from that area during the 1600s. Pirates have also used the straits as a haven from which to attack and plunder their victims.

When the Sunda Straight did not appear so quickly, I remembered Sumatra was the fifth largest island in the world, stretching across the equator for a thousand miles. I had purposely sat on the left side of the plane in order to have a bird's eye view of Krakatoa, the infamous volcano, which erupted in 1883, sending out the loudest bang in history. According to historical records, Krakatoa erupted so explosively that it was heard on Rodriguez Island in the Indian Ocean, more than twelve thousand miles away. The police chief on that island reported hearing a boom that sounded like "heavy guns from a battleship in the east."

As the plane passed to the left side of Krakatoa, I noticed a new bulge, called Anak Krakatoa (the child of Krakatoa), which was developing inside the main crater. Belching smoke was periodically escaping from the active crater, a reminder of just how catastrophic Krakatoa's explosions were when it erupted in 1883. When it exploded, its core fell back into the belly of the crater, causing towering tsunamis over 120 feet high. It killed over thirty-six thousand people and destroyed 165 villages as it wreaked havoc along the coasts of Java and Sumatra. Worldwide, it affected atmospheric conditions, and its ashes circled the world in a westerly direction. Even now, Anak Krakatoa continues to grumble. White smoke is a sign of normal volcanic activity. Grey smoke means beware!

As the plane neared Jakarta, I could see that the population sprawl of such large cities as Merak and Serang left no distinguishing line between them and Jakarta, sometimes called the "Big Durian." It is said that a person either loves Jakarta or hates it. Jakarta embraces both the good and the bad of Indonesia.

After I deplaned, I quickly found a taxi to the Peace Corps office and hostel next to the Hotel Indonesia, at that time one of the capital's few hotels with Western conveniences. The proximity of the Peace Corps office to the hotel was both good and bad, especially for those of us who craved Western desserts that we had only dreamed of at our various remote coaching locations. The restaurant there provided a relaxing atmosphere to meet over a cup of Javanese coffee, cold drinks, hamburgers, and malts. It was also one of the few sources of ice cream in the entire country. One volunteer, Ken Hollis, so longed for anything ice cream that he spent his entire clothing allowance for the next year on sundaes and malts at the Hotel Indonesia. The hotel did actually have some of the best ice cream in the world—at least, our world.

After fifty years, the hotel coffee shop has changed, but so have we volunteers who are now in our seventies. In fact, by 2011, when I returned to Indonesia, the Hotel Indonesia stood alongside many five-star hotels that defined the Jakarta skyline. Only the foundation of the coffee shop remains as part of the hotel's garden and waterfall area, and the restaurant boasts fine Indonesian and European cuisine. I searched carefully for remains of the old hotel while a helpful hotel manager accompanied me, explaining the hotel's evolution into the twenty-first century. After some nostalgic scouting, I was disappointed. I was unable to locate any remaining structures of the original hotel, the building for the Peace Corps offices, or "our" coffee shop beside the pool.

Resigned to the reality of change, my wife and I decided to enter the posh restaurant and have a chocolate malt for old time's sake. The only thing that had not changed was that I still wondered if I could afford to eat in the restaurant. There were polished, well-lit buffet serving stations for all kinds of ethnic-themed foods. The dessert station was popular, of course. With soft music in the background and gracious hostesses attending to the guests, I knew that this hotel certainly catered to the well-to-do and the educated. Seated behind me was a lunch group of professional men who were discussing ideas for expanding programs at their university. Before we were even seated, I asked if it were possible for us to order just chocolate malts. "Of course," responded the hostess, as she welcomed us into the dining area.

And then, to my shock and heartfelt surprise, my mouth fell open as I stared at two life-sized black-and-white pictures taken in the early sixties of President Sukarno standing with President John F. Kennedy. The enlarged 1960s photographs, the main focus of the restaurant decor, covered the entire west wall of the restaurant. Seated just below the historical photographs and marveling at life's twists and turns because of my Peace Corps years, my wife and I thoroughly enjoyed our chocolate malts.

Fifty years earlier, when I walked into the first reunion at the Peace Corps' hostel, I saw animated friends chattering away. The atmosphere seemed like a high school reunion, with Peace Corps volunteers sharing stories and experiences from their first six months in Indonesia.

The next two days were busy. Medical examinations and required written reports dulled our excitement. On November 22, however, we packed into a bus headed for a retreat center located in Bogor. Traveling through the Puncak Pass, we were in some of the most beautiful scenery of West Java. Narrow, winding roads ushered us through scenic tea plantations and terraced rice fields at altitudes over four thousand feet. This change in altitude and spectacular scenery also brought a welcomed change in temperature.

The bus eventually veered away from the main road to Bandung onto a small gravel road that led to a conference building surrounded by cottages with beautiful gardens overlooking hillside tea plantations. What a magnificent location for our first Peace Corps conference. Soon after breakfast the next morning, we gathered for our first discussion session. The discussion topic of why the Peace Corps was in Indonesia stimulated lively responses and provided an arena for discussion, so essential for a healthy attitude in dealing with the day-to-day challenges we all faced. Some felt that our coaching and ultimate success at the Olympics would define us. Others had come to believe that our daily living and relationships with the Indonesians would be our far-reaching legacy.

As the discussions continued, Dave Burgess, a career diplomat and the director of our Peace Corps project, walked quietly into the room. Leaning against the doorpost as he thoughtfully listened to the give-and-take, candid conversation, he didn't throw out his normally upbeat, "Good morning, guys!" Usually very vivacious and articulate, with a lot to say, he simply listened. At last, we gave him an opportunity to speak. Only then did I notice the anguished look that consumed his pale face. After a brief pause, Dave took a deep breath and announced directly and painfully, "The president of the United States has been assassinated."

A quiet hush of disbelief permeated the room as we all tried to make sense of Dave's announcement. I felt as if the wind had been knocked out of me. Others cried. Some found comfort in each other. Being in total shock, we reeled in confusion. How could this be? Just six months previously, we had proudly claimed our place in history as the second Peace Corps group to meet President Kennedy at the White House in the Rose Garden. Again, we recalled how he had warmly and proudly welcomed us and wished us the best as we represented the United States in Indonesia. He had shaken hands with each one of us and personally asked what sport we coached. I even recalled that there was evidence of children at the White House. His young children, John and Caroline, who were three and five years old at the time, had left toys strewn on the grass of the Rose Garden. Just six months previously! And suddenly we were the last Peace Corps contingent ever to meet him.

Shaken and yet solid, Mr. Dave Burgess encouraged each of us to seek the strength of his or her own faith and to find solace in the beautiful gardens surrounding the conference center. It was a long, painful day.

President Kennedy's assassination was a powerful and catastrophic event that modern history would sadly record as a loud bang (one of the loudest) heard around the world. Due to modern technology, that bang would not only resonate in the lives of Americans but in the lives of people throughout the world. Almost anyone, including our Indonesian staff who lived during the 1960s, can recall what he or she was doing on November 22, 1963, when the news arrived: "President Kennedy has been assassinated."

Krakatoa brought tremendous physical destruction to mankind, both in lives lost and property destroyed. Kennedy's death brought a different destruction—an attack on hope and the positive spirit that spawned President Kennedy's dream for the Peace Corps. Yes, these were powerful events that shocked the world, and for the moment, we seventeen volunteers were shattered. We were stranded in Indonesia with the challenge to regroup, recommit, and carry on because that's what President Kennedy challenged us to. He proudly served the country he loved; we would attempt to follow in his footsteps.

15

The Dinner Invitation

I was still reeling emotionally from the news of President Kennedy's assassination as I exited the DC-3 on my return to Palembang from the weeklong Peace Corps conference in Jakarta and Bogor. It seemed that much of my world had changed in just one week. Jim had transferred to Medan to coach in a thriving track program. I was returning to Palembang to live alone. The loneliness, in fact, was intensified because I was on the other side of world at the time of Kennedy's assassination.

On the other hand, as the DC-3 landed in the muggy heat of the South Sumatran afternoon, much remained the same. I felt refreshed and excited about arriving at my home base to continue my coaching and teaching commitments. From the airport, I took a bemo, one of those "public forms of transportation" so generic to many third-world countries. At the time, our bemos were World War II jeeps converted into taxis with wooden sides and bench seats designed to transport about six people. But why travel comfortably when the driver could pack up to twelve passengers with some hanging off the back and sides? Besides, the cramped quarters provided a perfect environment for working pickpockets. In any case, as we drove the familiar Sudirman Boulevard, I felt a comfort and peace. This was where I belonged in Indonesia.

Just prior to the Peace Corps conference, I had moved into the general's house, the same general who had appointed himself "guardian of the punch bowl" at the Pusri Fertilizer gala night. So when the bemo dropped me off at the post office upon my return from the Peace Corps conference, I walked the remaining two miles to my new "digs" with a sense of anticipation. The walk to this home took me through a comfortable residential neighborhood that was in the vicinity of the governor's mansion.

As I walked into the house and then toward the cottage provided for us, I imagined Jim calling out, "Hey, Paul! What's happening?" Instead, the only friendly noises came from children playing throughout their house. My bedroom was quiet and simply furnished, just as I had left it, with two single beds, two dressers, and a small writing desk in the corner. Seeing the desk covered with school work reminded me that I needed to turn my attention to my English literature courses.

On top of a stack of student work, I noticed a small envelope with my name scrawled across the front of it. Thinking it might be from the Gonia's with news of their sick son, Mark, I quickly opened it and found, instead, an invitation to Pak Benteng's house for dinner the following Friday evening.

Several months previously, I had met Pak Benteng at a gathering for prominent citizens in Palembang. Pak had seemed friendly and talked incessantly about his student days at Purdue University in the United States. I remembered that we had spent time comparing the Indonesian system of education with that of the United States. Pak Benteng felt that the United States' system was too lenient and did not demand enough discipline and work from its students. I also recalled that he talked about working for Shell Oil Company, a job that provided him sufficient income to maintain a home in an older, established suburb of Palembang near the governor's mansion. Prior to the 1948 uprising, the area had been a Dutch enclave, and Pak Benteng had purchased the home from a Dutch expatriate.

With invitation and address in hand the next Friday evening, I decided to walk to Pak's home since it was in the vicinity of the general's home. I knocked on the front door several times before a servant, who was wearing a black sarong and a white serving coat, politely greeted me with, "*Selamat malam* (Good evening), and nervously escorted me into the formal sitting room. The ornate sitting room could have been right out of an interior decorating book featuring the Dutch colonial period. The wallpaper depicted Dutch pastoral hunting scenes. The chairs and table were made from dark teak wood. I sat marveling at the exquisite décor until Pak and Ibu walked into the room to formally greet me. I sensed right away that this would not be a casual backyard barbeque. There were no welcoming smiles on their faces, quite a contrast to the typical warm Indonesian hospitality. In fact, I wondered if my arrival had interrupted a serious conversation. As I stood up to shake hands with Pak, he introduced me to his lovely wife, who was dressed in a traditional Indonesian sarong and blouse.

Along with the formal introductions and greetings, I sensed a slight coldness in Pak's voice and mannerisms. We continued the polite, formal conversation, however, until the servant announced that dinner was ready in the dining room. While we were awaiting the first course, Pak suddenly turned the congenial, light talk to topics that involved current politics. In an attempt to avoid a political discussion so early in the visit, I tried politely to explain to Pak that the Peace Corps strongly advised volunteers not to engage with the host nationals on any topics dealing with religion or politics. Pak, however, with a flushed face and coldness in his voice, continued to direct the conversation to politically-charged topics, such as the United States' presence in Viet Nam, the tensions between Indonesia and British-backed Malaysia, and the Peace Corps' presence in Indonesia. As we ate the cabbage salad, I thought to myself, "This is only the first course, and I have dodged some heated questions. I wonder what else will be on my plate tonight."

Eventually, Pak posed the question that I should have known was coming. "Mr. Paul, why are you here in Indonesia, especially teaching at the University of Sriwidjaja?"

I briefly explained the concept of the Peace Corps as proposed in President Kennedy's inaugural address in 1960. And then I added, "He spoke to Americans, especially the young, with his challenge: 'Ask not what your country can do for you; ask what you can do for your country.'" I continued, "Pak, do you know the next sentence that followed Kennedy's challenge? President Kennedy also said, 'My fellow citizens of the world: ask not what America will do for you, but what together we can do for the freedom of man.'

"President Kennedy's speech captures the spirit that inspired me to commit myself to two years here. The Olympic Games bring many nations of the world together, and I want to do my part to make sure Indonesian athletes will march in the opening ceremonies in Tokyo, Japan. President Sukarno asked President Kennedy to send coaches. Do you realize that President Sukarno is also welcoming a second contingent of volunteers next year that will include English teachers as well as coaches? Actually, with my background and experience, I represent both groups. Pak, we are volunteers and are paid very little. We do not have political agendas, except to share who we are and what skills we have learned."

Pak remained quiet after my answer but then impatiently said, "Ya, ya. But isn't your training and background in sports? Why are you teaching English at the university to students in the education department?" I realized that the arrival of the main course did not derail Pak's probing questions, so I uncomfortably continued to answer.

"Pak, my academic degree and graduate work are in English literature. I was selected to coach Indonesian athletes because of my athletic skills and my collegiate participation in weight training and track and field events. The KOGOR has not provided me enough coaching hours to keep me busy, so I gladly accepted the teaching opportunity at the University of Sriwidjaja when Rektor Hardjono asked me to take Pak Domes' English courses when he retired and returned to New Zealand.

Once again, my answers appeased Pak only momentarily, even though his face belied his frustration and anger. The arrival of dessert provided a respite from his probing. It was a great dinner, but I was not used to such lack of hospitality, especially in Indonesia, where visits often span hours filled with warm-hearted conversation. It seemed as if Pak had broken the code of hospitality by focusing on politics.

His last question, however, revealed his motive for inviting me to his home. "When teaching English literature to your university classes, do you attempt, in any way, to indoctrinate your students with Western, capitalistic ideas?" It was at this point that I began to understand Pak's real reason for the dinner invitation. His distant behavior, his lack of eye contact, and his leading questions all stemmed from his political stance and apparent involvement in Indonesia's turbulent politics.

Although disappointed, I answered his last question with polite assertiveness. "The FKIP (education department) students whom I teach follow a set curriculum designed by the rektor and her staff of educators. This course was established long before I arrived in Palembang. Furthermore, as an English teacher, I have always attempted to teach as objectively from the literary text as possible and certainly not from any political agenda."

I politely suggested that it was time for me to leave. Pak, with a twisted smile on his chagrined face, ignored me and pursued, "Paul, what do you think of the young communists causing the closure of the USIS libraries throughout Indonesia, especially the larger branches in Jakarta and Bandung?" I had just returned from Jakarta, where I witnessed a mindless mob gut the library and set fire to a mountain of books used by university students. I knew what Pak was talking about, and I remembered my fear as I stood on the outer perimeter watching the destruction.

"Pak," I replied, "I was recently there in Jakarta when the communist youth (PKI) destroyed the library. I stood in fear as the mob destroyed textbooks, classic literature, and resource materials. I heard them chanting, 'Down with America! Crush Malaysia! Destroy all Western ideas!' My fear was not only for my life, but for the results of censorship against freedom of thought and ideas. Yes, the thousands of educational books were a gift from the United States, but do you really believe they were tools of Western propaganda? The Indonesian students need books for their education that the system cannot provide. You must be aware of that. Why did you attend Purdue? Surely there are no threats in the technical and scientific books on farming, nursing, and medicine. What a hopeless and futile perspective to believe that an idea can be destroyed by burning books."

Pak responded angrily, "Mr. Paul, Indonesian students don't need books and ideas from the West."

I, in turn, answered, "Pak, in a world that is becoming more technical every day, don't you want Indonesian students to have a balanced education by reaching for the best from the West and the East? Don't you think that a student has a better opportunity to succeed if he or she has been exposed to both? Pak, as you must realize, books of any kind are difficult to obtain in Indonesia. The closing of the USIS libraries has made it impossible for thousands of Indonesian students to read and to prepare for their final examinations. As a result, thousands will not be able to complete their degrees. Is that what you want, Pak?"

Pak vehemently replied, "Students from the PKI are needed for Indonesia's revolution against the Old Forces." All pretense of polite reserve vanished as his eyes darkened and his lower jaw jutted out. "You better leave the university now or something will happen to you!"

A moment of dreaded silence filled the air as he realized what he had said in anger. He had gone too far. I politely said my goodbyes and thanked Ibu, who looked stunned, for her delicious dinner.

I walked home with Pak's threat ringing in my ears but with an added resolve to continue teaching my courses at the university.

16

Strange Occurrences

Artist: Ross Miller

The folklore of every culture throughout the world has tales of strange occurrences, eerie sightings, and mysterious happenings that entertain and seek to explain about our human existence and the nature around us. The Scots have long sought to explain the Loch Ness Monster, a possible gigantic sea slug. Sightings of the Abominable Snowman shroud the mysterious lore of the Himalayas. In California, there is the popular legend of Bigfoot. Somehow, in Palembang, Sumatra, the local people relate a more recent tale of a mysterious reappearing World

War II white ambulance that periodically materializes at the old Dutch graveyard with the ghosts of five Australian nurses who were killed during the Japanese occupation.

There are also older tales of dark powers that control entire villages in Indonesia, which has always been a land of witchdoctors, strange occurrences, and mysterious happenings. In the 1960s, witchdoctors still practiced their dark arts on Indonesia's many tribal groups. Realizing the controlling influences of witchcraft, President Sukarno banned witchdoctors from practicing their black trade. For most Westerners in the twenty-first century, this topic of strange occurrences becomes incredulous, is often dismissed as nonacademic, and is considered unscientific or unsophisticated.

I saw and experienced, however, events that defied explanation. On the outskirts of Bandung, the second largest city in Indonesia, I witnessed a man walk the length of a bed of hot coals stretching ten feet long and three feet wide without burning his feet. In Surabaya, I witnessed a truck slam into a horse-drawn hay cart with children hanging off the back and sides. I saw children catapulted through the air. The impact of the collision of the truck crashing into the hay cart could be heard a block away as people began running toward the accident. Horrified, I expected the children to be injured or dead. However, after lying on the ground briefly, all the children, one by one, simply got up and ran away as though nothing had ever happened. Children should have died in that accident, but none did. They did not even limp away!

Another puzzling incident for me happened when I visited one my students named Armen. My gracious university students often found various ways to welcome me into their lives. Armen, one of my English literature students, once said, "Mr. Paul, if you are ever out in the rural area of Sungaigerong, please stop to visit me and my family." The invitation itself was a rich treasure of hospitality, especially to a lonely Peace Corps volunteer seeking his place in Indonesian culture. I had tucked that invitation away in my mind.

Months later, I found myself in that area, having just finished a coaching clinic in track at a secondary school near the Musi River. I gathered the students around to conclude the clinic and to say goodbye. It was getting late, and I still had a long distance to go before I got home. I collected my coaching gear, putting my measuring tape, discus, ten-pound shot put, and students' performance charts into my sturdy backpack, along with my trusty flashlight used for traveling jungle roads. With the joyful sounds of the students saying, "Goodbye, Mr. Paul! Goodbye, Mr. Paul!" ringing in my ears, I started down a dark, deserted dirt road that would take me the twelve kilometers back to Palembang. It was comforting to know that I was riding a reliable motorbike now that the infamous "bike from hell" was repaired. I was able to conduct track clinics throughout the provinces of Palembang without the fear of being stranded.

As I gathered my thoughts to the purring of the motorbike, I remembered Armen saying that his house was along the road not too far from the secondary school where I had just spent the afternoon. Even though Armen didn't know I was in the vicinity, I decided to pop in for a quick visit with his family. I smiled in realizing that I had friends even in rural Indonesia and that I had already internalized the Indonesian social etiquette allowing one to stop for a visit unannounced. How nice to maneuver so comfortably in the Indonesian way of life! I did, however, wonder if it would be too late in the day, too close to the family's dinnertime.

Approaching a clearing cut away from the dense jungle, I came across a small cluster of wooden houses built on stilts in a semi-circle facing the road. I recalled Armen giving me his address: "Next to the market, which is also the post office." I parked my motorbike at the side of the market and then knocked several times on a flimsy door. To my surprise, Armen came to the door, greeting me as though he had been anticipating me, and warmly said, "Mr. Paul, we are glad you are here. Please come in. We have been expecting you for dinner and have set a place at the table especially for you." After I greeted the whole family in the Indonesian style of *selamant malam,* I noticed that, sure enough, there was an empty chair at the table with an additional Indonesian place setting of the typical bowl and tin spoon. Guess who was coming for dinner! They knew, but I didn't! How did they know?

It was a great visit. Complementing the simple meal of fish from the Musi River, locally grown rice, and fruit for dessert, we enjoyed lively conversation around the table. The chatter included events at school and the Indonesian economy. It became more animated when the children started to share the local Sumatran news about the man-eating tiger that was recently killed as it scavenged through the trash behind their village market. The children's bright, brown eyes smiled with delight as they saw fear creep into my face. I tried to bluff my way out of this by "playing it cool" and not overreacting. The children, however, were not deceived. In fact, they knew uncannily that I was frightened, at least a little. To be honest, my American literature mind drifted to the story of Ichabod Crane and the headless horseman who terrorized another sleepy, remote village.

So to match their Sumatran story, I told of the python I had recently run over while riding my bike one moonless evening along a remote jungle road. The jungle seemed even darker because the light on the front of my bike was broken. The children's eyes opened wide to greet my scary story: "At first, I did not notice the snake slithering across the entire width of the dirt road. Nor could I see that it was as big around as your father's thigh. Only as a jeep approached from the opposite direction did its lights reveal to me that I was just about to collide with the outstretched monster, which spanned the ten-foot width of the road such that I could not see its head or tail." The children squealed with fear and delight as my *bloop! bloop!* described the sound of the bike crossing over the python. There was more childish laughter as I confessed that I had put both feet on the handlebars of the bike as the *bloop! bloop!* mixed with the sounds of the jungle. And, no, I did not look back as I raced away!

As I said my *selamat tinggal* (goodbye), I realized I was leaving later than I had expected, but I savored the warmth of a gracious family whose wealth was in their love for one another and who could unabashedly welcome a stranger. This was really the essence of the Peace Corps mission, people meeting people.

Of course, as I left, I had laughed with Armen's family as they waved goodbye and jokingly warned, "Watch out for tigers, Mr. Paul! Watch out for tigers!" And, yes, there was the music of the children's chatter and squeals that faded as I started my motorbike. In contrast to the warmth of the family and the limited soft lights from the cluster of homes, the darkness of the jungle beyond the village loomed between home and me.

Twenty minutes later, with my eyes adjusted to the darkness of the jungle, I could see a field with tall grass on my right side and dense jungle on my left. Due to the many potholes in the mud road, I could not travel very fast, in spite of the eerie atmosphere. Trying carefully to dodge the huge holes caused by the rainy season, I suddenly noticed out of the corner of my right eye that something large was moving quickly through the tall grass parallel to me. I became concerned when the grass continued to part in an undulating pattern. Soon panic knocked at my very core, with my heart racing and chills creeping down my spine. This was no horror movie that I could turn off! In an attempt to get away from whatever it was, I opened the throttle to full speed, hoping to escape, although I realized that with a Ducati 50cc I could not outdistance an attacker. Whatever it was, it was gaining on me, running diagonally toward the road and toward me! Recalling the children's story earlier in the evening, I feared it was a Sumatran tiger stalking its prey.

Suddenly, the animal broke through the tall grass and onto the road as I spotted it directly in front of my bike and heard its guttural growling. It happened so quickly that I did not have a chance to avoid the collision. The sound of the impact was like that of a large melon being split in half by an axe. Then the animal's body plummeted into the ditch at the side of the road as dying sounds of shrilling and screeching filled the night air with ominous cries. Its head smashed, it lay on its back with is claws and legs twitching in the night air.

Then all ceased, and the quietness left me stunned. Finding the motorbike damaged and the headlight broken, I switched off the engine and reached into my backpack for the flashlight in order to see what I had hit. It wasn't a Sumatran tiger, like I had feared. Instead, I was staring at a giant field rat with a torso the size of a German shepherd. Its stocky legs, sharp claws, and snout, out of which protruded sharp teeth, gave it a fearsome appearance, like a hideous monster from a horror movie. Feeling sick at the sight of blood and guts smeared over the front of the bike and smelling the stench permeating the air, I sat down to get control of myself. My legs were weak and nausea overwhelmed me. The sudden quietness, following the violent death of the field rat, created a surreal setting. The putrid smell still hovered. I had to escape.

Examining the front of my motorbike, I discovered the front fender smashed against the front tire, a problem I easily fixed. Then I turned on the ignition and attempted to kick-start the bike. After several anxious moments, the bike started to purr again. Except for the front headlight not working, the bike seemed ready for the journey home. So, holding my flashlight in my left hand and using my right for steering and the throttle, I continued my way toward Palembang.

In a few minutes, I would be approaching a dark T-junction with a right turn heading toward Palembang and the left turn leading to Pusri, the chemical fertilizer plant where I had danced with President Sukarno's daughter (the future president of Indonesia) at the gala opening. Along that stretch of road to the Pusri plant, there was a security gatehouse for both the factory and the housing compound for expatriates working for the company.

As I slowed the bike down to make the right turn to Palembang, six figures throwing rocks and sticks in my direction suddenly emerged from the cover of the jungle. Was this for real? Was I really under attack again? Dodging and blocking the barrage, I realized deep down that I was alone in facing a determined group of assailants. One rock eventually hit the gas tank with a frightening metallic thud. Another hit me just above my right ear. Everything seemed to grow blurry as I fought to keep myself from sinking into unconscious darkness. With survival upmost on my mind, I remembered to turn off the ignition and pull the bike down onto myself as a shield, but, at some point, I would have to get the bike off me in order to fight back or to run. The added weight of the ten-pound shot put and the discus in my backpack kept me from moving quickly. Meanwhile, rocks and sticks were coming from all directions while the attackers shouted the typical communist slogans: "US imperialist, go home! Crush US! Peace Corps, go home!" I remember thinking, "Is this what Pak Benteng had threatened?" I thought also of home. "My poor parents! Wait until they read about this in the news!"

Just when I felt there was no hope, the lights of an approaching car and the sound of its engine broke into the darkness, scattering my assailants into the jungle. A carload of four workers coming from the direction of the Pusri fertilizer plant on their way home to Palembang approached the intersection. I knew these had to be Pusri workers because of the tight security along the road and surrounding the plant, which was a potential "powder keg" in the hands of terrorists. The security guards kept careful records and watch on everyone going in and out of the fertilizer plant premises. No "joy riders" would be on that road. I knew these people were from the Pusri plant.

As this carload of workers reached the intersection to find me under attack and bleeding from my head and arms, they jumped out of their car and rushed to my aid with their flashlights and first aid kit. Fortunately, I had used the motorbike and my arms as a shield to protect myself. The men helped me to my feet and walked me over to the passenger side of the car, where they cleaned and bandaged my head and arms. The blood ceased, but not the shaking of my body or the chattering of my teeth. Seeing my condition, they offered me a ride back to Palembang. Since I hurt all over, part of me wanted to accept their offer.

Even in my weakened and fearful condition, however, I realized I could not yield to intimidation from those who wanted me out of the university and out of Indonesia. At this crucial turning point, I had to make a hard decision. If I gave into my fears and the bullying of the communists, I would also need to pack my bags and head home to the

United States immediately. I would not give in! Buoyed by thoughts of my grateful, dedicated students and the support of the rektor of the university for my teaching, my spirit rallied. I would not give in! After all, what could possibly go wrong now? Or so I thought! I wanted to continue the productive year deepening relationships with the Indonesian people, fanning the fire of my Indonesian students' desires to learn, and enjoying the beauty of Indonesia through travel. Right! I refused to be intimidated by an ideology that attempted to use hate and fear to capture the minds and souls of the Indonesian people—and me. So with my remaining strength, I lifted up my motorbike for the journey home.

I picked it up off the ground only to discover that the gas tank was smashed and both fenders were badly damaged. The men stood by to see if I could start the bike. Wow! It actually started! Thinking that I would be okay, the men left before I could really thank them. Suddenly, it was as though they had never been there.

Jumping ahead one week, I was still pondering the events of that horrendous evening and wanting to thank my rescuers. I returned to the security gate at the fertilizer plant to ask about the carload that had left the plant about eight o'clock the previous Wednesday night. The guards carefully checked their records to verify if any car had traveled down the road that only serviced the fertilizer plant employees. The guards remembered, however, that it had been, "a slow night last Wednesday." Careful scrutiny of their books revealed that no car, especially one loaded with four men, had left or entered the gate between six and nine. Even today I try to piece together the events of the evening, an evening of strange occurrences.

But back to the actual night at the T-junction. After picking up both my flashlight and the backpack off the ground, I was ready to start my final trek home, my Ithaca. I was so thankful to be alive! With my renewed determination, I felt there was now hope for the future. The ride would not be too long, but it did mean that the bike and I had still to climb a small hill before starting down a long straight road into the outskirts of Palembang and eventually home. After riding slowly and cautiously over the small hill, I was then ready for the faster descent into Palembang. Since the rest of the ride promised to be easier, hopefully without any unforeseeable problems, I started to rehearse in my mind all that had happened to me that evening, starting with Armen's unexpected welcome to his home, hitting the giant field rat the size of a large dog, and finally being attacked by six men on the road. All these strange occurrences were almost too much for my reeling mind to comprehend. I would certainly be more accepting of and sympathetic to my students' tales, such as the frequent one about a 1943 World War II vintage white ambulance parked in front of a Dutch graveyard.

All of a sudden, the light of awareness struck me. "Hey! This must be the road that runs past the old Dutch graveyard." As I approached, my left hand, which held the flashlight, began to shake as the beam of light revealed a white ambulance! My whole being, body and mind, screamed, "Help! How can this be?" As my heart raced, my eyes sought for reality. Trembling took over, and even my 1960s crew cut seemed to stand firmer on end. I could not believe this was happening to me.

In spite of all this panic, as I got closer, I noticed that the white vehicle was a 1960 Dodge ambulance rather than a World War II vintage vehicle. Keeping in survival mode, I tried to gather all the facts. Yes, it was a white ambulance but not of the 1943 vintage. Yes, it was in front of the graveyard, but where were the five nurses? Was this another strange occurrence? No! This was a practical joke carried out by bored locals! Did the joke work? Yes!

When I got home, my coworker sat in the small sitting room, playing cards. Glancing quickly between his card moves, he quipped, "Hey, Burghdorf. Where have you been? I've had a boring evening playing solitaire." His greeting left me speechless!

17

Too Sick for Comfort

"You were lying unconscious, face down on the bathroom tile floor with feces and vomit everywhere. Paul, believe me, you were not a pretty sight when I found you," reminisced Bob Gonia. "You were one sick man, and I knew I had to get you to emergency help immediately." Then, wishing not to say much more at my hospital bedside, Bob simply shook his head and smiled in affirmation. "You are going to be okay, buddy."

Evidently, I was so sick that my Indonesian family, fearing the worst—typhoid, maybe—had left me alone in the small cottage next to their house without getting me medical care. I was too ill to know what was happening. And I am not sure how long I lay delirious before Bob Gonia found me. Looking back at that time, I do not blame my Indonesian family, the second family with whom I stayed. They knew that contagious illnesses, such as cholera and dysentery, could spread quickly. I certainly did not want to expose anyone, especially my Indonesian family, to danger.

When I had missed an important meeting about sports for a group of young people, Bob thought it strange that I wasn't there, especially since I was the one who had called the meeting. Following his gut feelings, Bob drove quickly to my two-room cottage, where he found me unconscious. He covered me with an old blanket and packed me to his truck. Bob later explained that he covered me with the blanket because I was shivering and seemed cold. I, however, would not have blamed him for trying to keep the upholstery of his new truck clean. A man on an important mission, Bob drove quickly to the Musi River in order to catch the Stanvac ferry to the other side, where the British Stanvac Oil Company hospital was located.

Even though the hospital was built primarily for Stanvac employees, they rushed me immediately into the emergency room.

Coming out of my fog, I awakened to hear two British doctors discussing my condition in hushed tones. One ordered that I be placed immediately in a special unit for contagious diseases. The other added, "Paul could be within hours of dying. I'm deeply concerned that he is severely dehydrated, which certainly complicates his medical condition."

Throughout the hours that followed, I alternated helplessly in and out of consciousness. At some point, I again overheard several doctors in the hallway quietly discussing the seriousness of my condition. One doctor warned, "The next few hours will tell if Paul is going to live. If he doesn't show signs of improvement soon, we will have to operate."

Frightened at the prospect of dying and not having any family near, I lay there helplessly. Too weak to respond physically to my predicament, my spirit rallied enough to mumble, "God, please heal my sick and wasted body, if it is your will." Tears moistened my cheeks as I sensed God's love and His presence in that lonely hospital room. I seemed to hear, "Paul, I created you, and I am the great physician. I paid a great price for you, and I am not going to let you die. I love you, and I am not finished with you yet. Paul, do you trust me?" I clung to my favorite Scripture verse: "I know the plans I have for you," declares the Lord, "plans to prosper you and not to harm you, plans to give you hope and a future" (Jeremiah 29:11, NIV). With the hope of His promise and a deep sense of His hand on my life, I made a promise that night to God that if I were ever given opportunity to help missionaries—like Bob Gonia, who helped to save my life—I would gladly do it.

Many years later, twenty, in fact, God graciously and generously held me to my promise. How quickly we make promises in times of emergency. How easily we forget those promises when we are busy with a comfortable life. My wife and I, along with our children, were living in Kijabe, Kenya, and working at Rift Valley Academy as English teachers and dorm parents in the 1980s. More than four hundred students, most of them the children of missionaries, came from many African countries to study an American curriculum, to continue their immersion in African culture, and to experience a full and supportive boarding school program. Once again, I was overseas and enjoying my teaching and coaching opportunities and interacting with marvelous students. Frequently, I would treat the family to lunch in the school dining hall and to a lively time casually socializing with students whose parents were working with many Christian mission organizations throughout Africa. The spectrum of their jobs was mind-boggling and inspiring. There were the ones who shared their faith through evangelism, education, and Bible teaching. Others worked in construction, on water projects, in translation and literacy work, and in hospitals and clinics as doctors and nurses. I was regularly inspired to hear about the significant and sacrificial work in which my students' parents were involved.

One day as I was leaving the dining hall and chatting with one of my favorite seniors, I happened to mention that a missionary named Bob Gonia had helped to save my life in Indonesia in the 1960s. When I mentioned Bob's name, my student came to an abrupt stop, exclaiming, "Bob Gonia was my dad's best friend at the University of Tennessee." Like a missing puzzle piece that I had spent days trying to find, my life story suddenly came together. As only God could orchestrate, He kept me to my promise made to Him on my hospital bed in Palembang, Indonesia, in 1963. What could be clearer? I had the high calling to teach the sons and daughters of missionaries out of gratitude for the fullness of life God had granted me. To top it off, I was thoroughly enjoying working with the missionaries' priceless treasures, their children.

Back at the hospital that night in 1963, I was able to rest with a deep confidence that God would see me through the challenge of the next few hours. And then within a few days, I was able to keep down food and water as I turned the corner toward recovery.

If there is any joy in being sick, it comes when a patient can have visitors. The first visitors to make the long trek to Stanvac Hospital were friends from the church where Bob Gonia had alerted them to my condition. Mr. and Mrs. Ellmaker provided practical support, especially when Mrs. Ellmaker wrote a letter to my family in California detailing what had happened to me and assuring my parents that she would bring me to her home for my initial time of recovery. Dear Marge even offered to wash my filthy clothes. Oh my! I wondered if I could ever look her straight in the face again.

Bob and Pat Gonia came with their two lovely children. Bob had already confided in me, while on our trip to the leper colony, that his two-year-old son, Mark, was dying of liver cancer. My heart ached again as I saw little Mark smiling at me from his mother's lap. Pat's eyes were worn and red, revealing her inner turmoil, and Bob fought back tears as he informed me that they would soon be returning to the United States for Mark's operation and the required follow-up radiation treatment. I marveled at this family who had sacrificed much to live out their life priorities. Lying in my hospital bed and gazing at this little family, I knew I would be forever grateful to Bob for saving my life and forever grieved because of Mark's fatal condition. Even to this day as I write this difficult chapter, I struggle with renewed phantoms of sadness and grief. I also carry deep respect for a man who lived out his faith courageously and honorably, and I am privileged that he had invested himself in me.

And then the day came when I looked up from my bed to see six of my students, with beaming faces, standing at the door, anxious to visit me and to bring news from other students at the university. They had made the long trip across the Musi River and over rough roads in crowded taxis converted from World War II jeeps just to see me. Their beautiful smiles and joyous laughter did much to rekindle my spirit and to further my healing process. "Please come back to teach us after the term break, Mr. Paul. Will you be at the university for the start of second semester? We want to read more of *Canterbury Tales,* especially if you will speak in Middle English again." As they left, with their happy chatter trailing behind them, I knew I was committed to returning to my teaching and coaching in Palembang.

18

A Trip to Paradise— Third Class

Artist: Ross Miller

Upon hearing that the doctors had released me from Stanvac Hospital and that I was exercising rigorously each day, Dr. Wukasch, the Peace Corps doctor in Jakarta, responded, "Paul, it sounds as if you are doing just fine. You have accumulated some leave days from the Peace Corps. Why don't you use them during your term break from the university to vacation and rest in Bali? Stop by Jakarta for a medical exam on your way to Bali. And don't forget your medical records."

"Go!" encouraged Bob Gonia. "What a great opportunity to see Bali. Take the public transportation from Palembang to Bali, and you will have a fantastic eight-hundred-mile adventure crossing Java before you eventually reach Bali. Why don't you take a friend, at least part of the way?"

I immediately thought of King, who was the judo heavy weight champion of Palembang. We had worked together to establish a strength program for judo and track weight events, such as the shot put and discus. A goliath of an athlete, King was six foot two and weighed two hundred and fifty pounds. I knew he was heading to Bandung to compete in the national judo finals of Indonesia and suggested that we team up. We would travel together to Bandung, stopping first for my medical exam in Jakarta. Then I would accompany him to Bandung to cheer him on at his competition.

Our adventure began one afternoon at the Palembang docks. In the sixties, Palembang had become one of Indonesia's main oil refinery ports from which the "black gold" was shipped throughout the world. Among the large modern tankers, however, was a crowded "rust bucket" passenger ship, *The Star*, which was transporting pilgrims who were headed to Mecca. *The Star* was a euphemistic name for a ship that had long since lost its luster. Its port of origin was the northern city of Medan, so when King and I boarded in Palembang, the ship was already overcrowded with pilgrims who were hunkered down for the long trip to Mecca. The more well-to-do passengers had already filled all sleeping quarters, and our third-class ticket bought us just space enough on the top deck to squeeze in with hundreds of pilgrims who had staked their claims before we even boarded the ship. President Kennedy would have been pleased to see his volunteers living "alongside the nationals of the country."

Every available space on deck was covered with tired bodies resting on each other, soiled mats, and dirty green army blankets. Even dirty rags tied in balls were used as headrests. Primarily men, they were dressed in their white robes. The struggle to survive the pilgrimage seemed endless for these people who were braving the long trip, the humid weather, and the relentless sun reflecting off the metal of the ship.

King and I were traveling only overnight on the ship toward Jakarta, but these pilgrims would travel many days over thousands of sea miles before they reached Saudi Arabia. We squeezed into enough space on the deck to unroll our one mat for sleeping, or at least what sleep we could catch.

King and I had claimed our space on the starboard side at the bow of the ship in order to see the volcanic remains of the once mighty Krakatoa that erupted in August 1883. By late afternoon, the ship was sailing past Anak (the child of) Krakatoa, the new land uprising from within the main crater which

I had spotted from the airplane on a previous trip to Jakarta. Closer this time, I could see that Anak was the temperamental offspring volcano that hurled glowing rocks and belched smoke and ash. An awesome sight!

We awoke the next morning with the call to prayer just prior to sunrise. And then dawn gave us our first peek of the silhouetted island of Java. As we rolled up the sleeping mat, it seemed as if we were joining the throng in their struggle to survive yet another day in their long pilgrimage. Vendors maneuvered through the crowd selling tea, bread, and biscuits as people squatted, drinking and speaking among themselves in hushed tones. Sunrise provided gentle warmth, but before long, the fiery sun became the only sure factor on the pilgrims' journey.

As the ship docked at the port city of Merak, Java, King and I joined the throng exiting the ship to stretch their legs and to buy food from dockside vendors before continuing their journey. The spicy aromas of food wrapped in banana leaves announced the food choices even before we could hear the vendors calling out, *"Daging Lada Hitam," "Nasi Goreng," "Opor Ayam,"* and *"Pisang Goreng."* These same aromas take on savory images when the Indonesian is translated into beef in black pepper sauce, spicy fried rice, chicken in coconut sauce, and fried bananas. Granted, these offerings were cooked at roadside huts in pans washed in polluted rivers, but the smells and sounds created colorful snippets of everyday life in Indonesia.

King and I, on the other hand, were rushing to catch a bus for Jakarta. Since King was so big, it was easy for him to push through the crowd. I trailed behind. Towering over everyone, he quickly located signs to the bus station, where we purchased our third-class tickets for the three-hour trip to Jakarta. Because the third-class tickets were cheap and popular, the buses were slow and always overcrowded. After we squeezed onto the bus past passengers carrying tied parcels, bundled produce, squawking chickens, and smelly ducks in woven reed cages, there was little room left for King and me—and our suitcases. Such tight bus conditions certainly allowed for close contact with Indonesians living out their daily lives. There was nothing easy about the trip; even the seats were hard boards.

As King and I entered the dilapidated bus, King found us a bench seat near the back. I left my small suitcase in the aisle and took the empty seat next to the window since it was becoming increasingly more difficult to breathe. Fresh air seemed in short supply due to the crowded conditions, the pungent odors of unwashed bodies, and even animal droppings. Add to this, people yelling, chickens squawking, and horns blaring from frustrated nearby motorists, and one can imagine the discomfort. A tired, elderly Indonesian woman, who was holding two white chickens upside down with their legs tied together, could not find an empty seat. Finally, she decided to sit on my suitcase.

This completes the picture that plays out in my mind even today. I have to say that I am glad I was young enough, poor enough, and inexperienced enough to buy that third-class ticket then.

Halfway through the trip, the bus made a scheduled rest stop—in other words, a toilet stop. This particular rest stop was conveniently located in front of food shops and souvenir stands. Behind the shops was the toilet, the polluted stream that separated open fields from a kampung that was a crowded, destitute area of the town with huts and shacks wedged together.

Passengers from the bus quickly ran toward the stream to relieve themselves behind the trees and bushes. King and I decided it would be better if one of us waited behind to watch the luggage until the other returned. Before I could say anything, King shot out of the bus and ran for the stream. When he returned, I immediately made my exit and ran toward the same stream.

As I started to relieve myself, I noticed two men approaching me, one from the front and the other from the rear. The one from the front asked for money while the other thrust his hand deep into the back pocket of my jeans. In disbelief, I yelled, *"Tidat ada uang! Tidat ada uang!"* (No money! No money!). Then, while the front thief approached me menacingly, I quickly backed into the man who was attempting to steal my wallet, swinging my left elbow into his head. As he fell to the ground, I had enough time to do a side kick with my right leg, knocking the second thief into the polluted stream.

Before I had time to congratulate myself, three more men were coming at me. I quickly yelled, "King!", but before I could say more, I saw three awkward-looking bodies flying toward the putrid water. In utter disarray, the remaining thieves ran toward the safety of their kampung. After his short display of speed and agility, King approached me saying, "Paul, you handled yourself well, but you still need to work on your side kicks." We both laughed and laughed, especially since the back pocket that the thief ripped off held no wallet. It was a wise idea that I had put my wallet into my front pocket, another traveling tip that King had taught me.

As we both got back on the bus, people were loudly cheering us. They seemed especially amazed at King's agility and power. He immediately became the hero of the bus as every little boy, with his bright, brown eyes, stared proudly at King. A few even wanted to sit on his lap. King was definitely the heavy weight judo champion of Palembang, maybe of Indonesia, or even of the world, in the eyes of those little boys.

Compared to the "excitement" at the rest stop, the remainder of the trip to Jakarta was uneventful, except for trying to exit the bus once we reached Jakarta. Even before the bus had stopped, a wave of determined people was attempting to board the bus just as we passengers were literally fighting to get off. The two waves of humanity collided at the doors of the bus. Again, King continued to call out, "Paul, follow me." After a few moments of pushing and shouting, we managed to get off the bus with my once-new suitcase sagging in the middle and with stains and rips rather than with the typical souvenir patches that Westerners proudly display after their traveling adventures. I also noticed that my other back pocket had been ripped off in the fray. As the bus drove away listing to one side, we watched in disbelief as people hanging on the sides of the bus were still trying to squeeze into it.

After a thorough medical examination by Dr. Wukasch at the Peace Corps headquarters in Jakarta, I was relieved to get a clean bill of health to continue my journey to Bali. More importantly, it meant that I could stay in Indonesia to continue my teaching and coaching. With a heavy weight off my shoulders, King and I decided to treat ourselves at the Hotel Indonesia with a hamburger and malt, our version of a celebration feast.

The next morning, we were at the Gambir train station, headed to Bandung. Even though we were tempted to take the faster, more comfortable Pakuan express train, we decided to keep within our budget by once again traveling third class. Once the train had left the Jakarta metropolis basin, the three-hour trip south to Bandung provided fresh, cool air and spectacular scenery. There seemed to be endless shades of green as we passed high mountains with terraced rice fields at the lower elevations and tea plantations and coffee farms at the higher elevations. The terra cotta color of the land contrasted with the hues of green foliage and the blue sky. The slower third-class train allowed us to savor the beauty of the land and the interactions of people living in villages along the tentacle of the railroad.

The third-class train also offered opportunities for us to be with the people. A moment in time offered me a poignant encounter with poverty and suffering. Into our crowded coach entered a young Indonesian mother with two small, emaciated children dressed in dirty rags. Her own tattered clothes and few possessions tied in an old cloth bag spoke loudly that she was poor. Quiet and hunched over, she stood with the children, balancing to the swaying motion of the train. When she looked up, my outstretch palm offered her my suitcase, the one that was already sagging from the bus trip. For the remainder of the trip, I was moved as I watched this woman caring for her children, even though she had nothing to offer them to eat. When I bought cooked rice for this little family from the food cart moving up the aisle, she quietly accepted it and shared it first with her children. Looking at me with dignity, she quietly responded, *"Terima kasih"* (thank you). Ashamed that I had not offered more, *"Kembali"* (you are welcome), was my only reply.

Once in Bandung, King and I watched the mother exit along with the many passengers towing children, chickens, and produce. This time we were in no hurry to exit as we breathed in Bandung's cool, fresh air and made our way to the Peace Corps hostel.

On the starting day of the Indonesian heavyweight judo competition, the events began immediately after the judo master had explained the competition format and rules. King breezed through the first two bouts.

In the final bout on the second day, I feared King had met his match. He faced off with the champion of Bandung, who was surprisingly taller and heavier than King. The men, both Indonesians of Chinese descent, seemed like giants compared to the average Indonesian. I thought to myself, "This does not look good for King. I have never seen King face an opponent bigger than he is." They provided quite a show as they attempted to throw each other to the mat. Grappling to gain the advantage, they seemed like two rams with their horns locked. As the minutes ticked away, there was no decisive winner. The Bandung champion's weight and height seemed to have the edge. In the end, however, King's agility, strength, and keen thinking propelled him to victory as he eventually pinned his opponent to the mat and claimed the title. Of course, I was proud to stand in his shadow during the victory celebrations, but I felt lonely to part with my co-traveler as he headed back to Palembang and I continued my trip to Bali.

Wanting to see the Borobudur Buddhist Temple, I caught a train to Yogyakarta. This time, I traveled without King, but I joined some friendly Australians from the judo match who also were traveling to "Yogya" in order to see Borobudur, which is considered to be one of the "seven wonders of the world," along with Angkar Wat. It is listed as a UNESCO World Heritage Site. Some people even believe that Borobudur is one of the greatest sights in Southeast Asia.

When I first saw Borobudur Temple, I was awestruck by its daunting size in contrast to the surrounding villages and emerald-green rice fields. From the top of the structure, visitors can see the nearby mighty Mount Merapi, a volcano that is still active. In fact, its most recent eruption, in 2010, brought destruction to villages between the mountain and Borobudur.

Borobudur is a pyramid structure of seven high terraces composed of fifty-five thousand square meters of lava rock, reaching, it seems, to the sky. To catch the Borobudur experience, I took the pilgrims' five-kilometer walk clockwise around the carved galleries on each of the seven terraces. The intricate carvings in the lava stone tell an ancient story of a pilgrim on a lifelong journey from his life on earth to a Buddhist heaven. Atop the Borobudur monument is a dome-shaped stupa surrounded by an additional seventy-two openwork stupas about ten feet high, each containing a statue of Buddha. People stretch their arms through the openings in an attempt to touch the statues inside for good luck. This eighth-century structure speaks of Indonesia's rich and varied history.

During the remainder of my trip across the island of Java, the train became my tour guide. It passed through Semarang and Surabuya, major population centers. And then the train seemed to crawl up mountainous regions and creep through villages in rural areas. Seated in the third-class section, I again enjoyed views of Indonesian villages where real-life scenes were acted out in front of me. I chuckled as I again watched little boys attempting to fly their colorful kites by copying all the movements of their older, experienced brothers. Time after time, they would run their hearts out with the string of the kite held in one hand, hoping to see the kites lift magically, only to turn and see them hanging limply just behind their heads.

The older boys took their kite flying more seriously, using their kites like instruments of war. They glued pieces of crushed glass onto their kite strings to rub against and cut their opponents' kite strings. The kites would whip through the sky, diving and dashing until the victor cut the strings of opponents and claimed their kites. Even the older boys would jump up and down joyously as they watched "the enemy's" kite flip-flopping to the ground. The only trophies awarded in those competitions were the kites themselves.

The living pictorial of Indonesian life continued through the windows of the train. There were children dressed in their blue school uniforms heading to school. Wearing a traditional straw hat, an old man, wrinkled from time and the heat of the sun, hobbled down a dirt path. Women, like beasts of burden, carried loads of produce to and from marketplaces. And then there was an elderly woman who carried her husband's lunch, wrapped in a red cloth, out to him as he tended his ducks in the water of the rice paddies. Here was the story: people living life in relationship to each other and in relationship with the earth from which they drew life.

It was also during these scenic times that my mind would travel back to my students in Palembang. They were my purpose for being in Indonesia. The students at the University of Sriwidjaja were in the teacher-training program and could possibly be teaching English one day in one of the rural schools I was passing. The athletes might also be fanning throughout the islands of Indonesia to share their coaching and physical fitness skills. I had a growing confidence that I would soon be ready to return to my students in Palembang.

Finally, the train stopped in Banyuwangi. Banyuwangi is a long word for a tiny town that is the ferry departure for Bali. The ferry, somewhat larger than a row boat, crossed the channel to Gilimanuk, Bali. A three-hour bus trip to Denpasar, the capital of Bali, brought me closer to my destination. Without wasting any more time in a crowded city, I hitchhiked to Kuta Beach in a dump truck that was being used in the construction of the new Ngurah Rai airport.

Ah, Kuta Beach! I was finally there after traveling thirteen hundred kilometers from Palembang to Bali—on a pilgrim ship, crowded buses, third-class trains, a make-shift ferry, and a friendly dump truck.

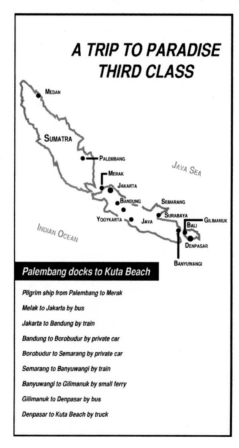

A TRIP TO PARADISE THIRD CLASS

MEDAN

SUMATRA

PALEMBANG

JAVA SEA

MERAK

JAKARTA

BANDUNG

SEMARANG

SURABAYA

GILIMANUK

YOGYAKARTA

JAVA

BALI

INDIAN OCEAN

DENPASAR

BANYUWANGI

Palembang docks to Kuta Beach

Pilgrim ship from Palembang to Merak

Melak to Jakarta by bus

Jakarta to Bandung by train

Bandung to Borobudur by private car

Borobudur to Semarang by private car

Semarang to Banyuwangi by train

Banyuwangi to Gilimanuk by small ferry

Gilimanuk to Denpasar by bus

Denpasar to Kuta Beach by truck

19

Paradise at Last

With my sagging suitcase in hand, I stopped to savor my first view of Kuta Beach from the steps of the cottage that was to be my retreat for the next three weeks. Set off about two hundred yards from the ocean, the Kuta Beach Hotel was the only structure on the entire white strand in the 1960s. Actually, the hotel was a cluster of about eight small, white cottages, some of which had panoramic views of Kuta Bay. Those cottages surrounded the open-air dining room and lounge, which served as the office for the hotel.

My cottage, one of the three less expensive one-room huts, was nestled behind the hotel kitchen, further back among the palm trees. It had a limited view of the beach, but boasted a fantastic hammock tied between two palm trees, which swayed in the afternoon breezes. Stretching out on the sisal netting to see if it could hold me, I chuckled aloud, "Dr. Wukasch and Bob Gonia must have ordered this just for me." The palm tree grove behind my hut stretched endlessly, so it basically served as a tropical screen for my privacy. Attached to the back of my hut was an outdoor bathroom that consisted of the toilet (two bricks and a hole) and a typical outdoor mandi used for hand-held showering. I could say that each cottage was decorated in a Balinese motif, but, in truth, I was in the real Bali surrounded with natural privacy.

It was hard to believe that this quiet, rustic hotel held a long and enduring history. It was constructed by a couple from California in the 1930s and must have truly offered an escape in paradise. I could imagine a lively atmosphere in which Dutch and international tourists wiled their evenings away around the bar, along the shoreline, or huddled by campfires prepared by the villagers to guide the outriggers through the opening in the reef. The subdued lights, perhaps lanterns or candles at that time, would have added to the laid-back atmosphere, not the nightclubs, congested traffic, and block upon block of tourist shops under the shadow of high-rise hotels that came later in the 1970s. This jewel of a small hotel was then neglected during the repressive Japanese occupation in the early 1940s. I could only imagine the sounds and events of that time period. Overgrown and deserted then, the hotel was eventually refurbished, in a limited way.

I was the only guest the first week. Later, two American pilots returning home from Viet Nam through Southeast Asia stayed for a few days. They were the only additional guests during my entire stay. Kuta Beach Hotel was truly a secluded retreat, ideal for anyone seeking physical and spiritual recuperation.

Once I was checked in, it didn't take me long to head down to the shoreline to savor this hidden corner of paradise. When I walked down to the surf, I noticed there were very few people on the beach. Surfers and tourists would come in the 1970s, but "my" Kuta was void of people, except for local fishermen mending their nets and tending their prows. Perhaps it was like what Waikiki Beach must have been decades before it became a crowded tourist attraction.

For a few pensive moments, I sat down in the virgin sand, watching the turquoise-blue water play tag with the shore. Kuta Beach was definitely the place where I wanted to recuperate for three weeks, enjoying the brilliant sunsets, the movements of the tide, and the cooling afternoon trade winds.

I walked back to the hotel to finalize details with the manager, who assured me that the hammock came with the room. Fantastic! Now I had two places to dream, one in my small cottage and the other in my hammock. In addition to the room, breakfast and dinner were included.

The first night, I fell asleep reading *Lord Jim*, a novel that takes place in Southeast Asia. The book parallels the life of Joseph Conrad in his search to find himself as he sailed from Marseilles to Malaysia. Hm! Perhaps I could also see myself in this adventure. Needless to say, I didn't read much of *Lord Jim* that night because of the awkwardness of handling a flashlight with my right hand while trying to read. The generator shut down after ten o'clock.

What a healing break it was to wake up early each morning before breakfast to walk barefoot along the sandy strand from Kuta Beach to Legian. My footprints were often the first each morning to leave their signature on the pristine sand. Of course, this reflective time allowed me to consider the gift of life and how I would live out my values. My faith was strengthened as I quietly read my Bible. I looked back on the previous months and began to see purpose in what had happened to me.

Before breakfast, I would do short wind sprints on the fresh sand to build up my leg strength and endurance. I would often finish my morning exercises with pushups and sit-ups. By the time I had finished exercising, the aroma of rich, dark Indonesian coffee signaled that breakfast was ready in the dining room.

No pancakes and syrup for breakfast! I would usually have nasi goreng, which was almost as good as the rice dishes made by my Indonesian mother, Ibu Bahar. Of course, every morning started off with a cup of that strong, black Balinese blend grown at the higher, cooler elevations on Bali's coffee plantations.

The second cup of coffee would often find me sitting on the beach in just a pair of shorts, thinking and praying for God's guidance in my life. I struggled to know the purpose of my life, as many young people struggle. What were my priorities? There were many unanswered questions, but I knew then that I wanted to be of service to others in some capacity rather than to amass wealth and immerse myself in my own pleasure. I certainly realized, however, that there is nothing wrong with enjoying the pleasures of life, such as a retreat in Bali.

I was blessed to have majored in literature and to have taken time to listen to some fine authors as I recalled their stories. The short story, "How Much Land Does a Man Need," by Leo Tolstoy, has the protagonist running his heart out to acquire as much land as he can square off in one day. As the protagonist comes to the end of his run just at sunset, he falls dead. He gets as much land as he needs, enough to be buried. As I also pondered Henry David Thoreau's words: "I went to the woods to live life deliberately," I recognized that I did not want to end my life by gathering just "things." As I realized that my future held rich purposes for me, I was again gaining an excitement and confidence about life. I felt encouraged to face my nebulous future because I was anchored in the confidence that God held my life—for purpose.

Before lunch, I would often take a swim in the warm tropical waters of the bay. Each day, I noticed I was getting stronger, especially in swimming. For lunch, I would often buy locally-grown sliced pineapple from a beach vendor. What a life! For the rest of the afternoon, I would rest in the hammock sleeping, reading, or thinking. Often in the afternoon, the trade winds would come up, transforming a hot, humid day into one that was pleasant and comfortable. As my strength returned, I realized, however, that I was lonely for someone to share life with. Paradise could not be perfect if it were "all about me."

Occasionally, Indonesian young ladies from a nearby village strolled up the beach, carrying baskets of tropical fruit on their heads while wearing only sarong skirts. Believe me, I was not dreaming! The scenes were natural, beautiful, and innocent. In 1964, however, President Sukarno outlawed such topless fashions.

Frequently in the evenings, I joined the villagers in building bonfires on the sand to guide their outriggers home. The coral reef shielding the shore from high waves had a narrow opening that was approximately fifty feet wide. The villagers would build two fires that served as beacons pinpointing the location and width of the break in the reef. As the outriggers swept through the break toward the shore, the action began. The fishermen, villagers, and I would plunge into the water to seize the outriggers and carry them high onto the sand, safe from the rising tide. If the fishermen had been successful with their catch, they would celebrate their good fortune by giving a fish to everyone who helped. That included me. This was the ultimate Bali—living, working, and enjoying life alongside the villagers who also enjoyed me.

Along with my renewed vigor for life came a resurgence of my appetite. I would run with my prized fish to the cook at the hotel. Often I held my reward in both hands since it was big enough to feed several people. The cook would congratulate me as if I had actually caught the fish myself. I can still hear him saying, "Mr. Paul, I am going to cook you a delicious nasi goreng dinner with fish, better than any meal in the Denpasar restaurants." Sure enough, before too long, the cook and I were huddling around a chopping block table behind the kitchen, eating a "five-star" dinner and watching the final moments of a brilliant Balinese sunset. This symbiotic relationship with my providing the fish and the cook making the delicious fish dinner was a daily ritual, at least on the days when the fishermen returned through the reef with their bounty. Is there any wonder why I carried home with me changed values and an appreciation for the simple pleasures of life?

After the fishermen had packed up their outriggers and most of the villagers had left the beach, I would sit quietly on the shore sometimes, dreaming, ironically, about home thousands of miles away. Family and friends were often on my mind. Perhaps I should have heeded the advice from one expatriate: "Enjoy 'here' while you are here, because you can't have 'here' there."

When I returned to my cottage or hammock, sleep came quickly and peacefully. Unapologetically, this was the way most of my days and nights were spent in paradise.

There were times, however, when I wanted to be with people, so I hitchhiked in the back of a dump truck to Denpasar, or I would borrow the cook's black bicycle, which was always leaning against a palm tree, ready for an adventure. In Denpasar, I watched gamelan shows, collected Balinese art, or attended the famous Balinese monkey dance. The dance is usually performed by up to one hundred and fifty shirtless men wearing only black and white checkered cloths around their waists. They depict two troops of monkeys chattering as they fight to gain dominance. In mass, each loud group imitates aggressive monkey behavior as they sway and throw their arms up, moving forward and then falling backward.

Sometimes I regretted the time spent away from Kuta Beach and its quiet, serene atmosphere. I far preferred my corner of Bali over the "maddening crowd" of Denpasar. I did not have money for dining out, so I usually made it back to my hotel for dinner before the generator cut off at ten. After all, I had my own personal cook!

Three weeks is a short time in paradise, and it came to an end quickly. Little did I realize that I could never return to Kuta Beach as it was in the 1960s. For several short weeks, God's providence had allowed me to experience a simple, carefree existence, which, in turn, provided me with an opportunity to listen. I was a captive audience.

Soon I longed to return to Palembang to complete my contracts with the university and with KOGOR. I knew there would be rewarding but difficult times ahead in teaching and coaching. My ambivalent feelings resulted from my knowledge that the communists were stepping up their attacks against Americans living in the country. My commitment, however, spoke louder than my conflicted feelings. In fact, I realized that my commitment spoke louder to that growing person deep inside me than the raging sounds of angry demonstrators that still rang in my memory. I had a job to complete, people to serve, and a promise to keep.

Fifty years later, in 2011, my wife and I returned to Indonesia, only this time to teach at Bandung Alliance International School. Before starting our volunteer work at the school, I wanted to return to Bali and Kuta Beach, and my wife, Marilyn, wanted to check out this tropical paradise I had talked about for so many years.

This time, instead of hitchhiking a ride, we hired a taxi—one of the blue taxis—from the Bali Spirit Hotel in Ubud to Kuta Beach. As we rode along the narrow roads toward Kuta, the driver spoke about his love for Bali and how the island had unfortunately changed because of tourism. I remember him saying, "The Balinese people have always smiled from their hearts. Now, because of money brought in by tourism, they smile only from the face."

The driver maneuvered his blue cab down the crowded and twisted roads of Kuta Beach, where tourists, cars, and hawkers vied for space in their search for the elusive spirit of "old Bali." He left us off at the monument erected in honor of the people who were killed in the terrorist bombings of October 12, 2002. Over two hundred people from twenty-three different countries were killed, and more than three hundred were injured. The terrorist attack shattered Bali's vibrant tourist business. It took ten years before there were any encouraging signs that the tourists were returning. Bali's innocence and elusive spirit, however, were still missing.

I didn't recognize anything that looked even vaguely familiar at Kuta Beach. A maze of streets, shops, and restaurants crowded with tourists now stood where dirt paths had once led me to the beach. High-rise hotels and building cranes used to construct higher and bigger hotels dominated the strand. There was no white cottage anywhere.

After a frustrating morning of searching my memory, talking to hotel staff, and questioning older life guards along the busy strand, we eventually found the location of the old Kuta Beach Hotel, obliterated by progress and change. The remnants of the old hotel were behind the façade of a five star hotel and fifty years of progress. Next to a sparkling pool was a fashionable snack and bar area that I eventually realized had once been the lounge and kitchen where my cook had prepared my fish dinners.

Encouraged, we entered the main hotel and ascended the circular marble staircase leading to the reception desk. Surely a hotel manager would know the history of the property. Politely asking to speak to a supervisor, the young lady at the desk replied, "He is in a meeting and will not be available for half an hour."

"That's okay," I responded. "We will wait because we are seeking information about the old hotel that was once here and where I stayed fifty years ago."

"Well," she replied, "our manager works for the hotel chain and was transferred here only two years ago from another resort. He won't have any information. Besides, who cares about the old hotel when you have this exclusive Inna Resort?"

We suddenly realized that no one cared about the Kuta Beach of the past except the two of us. Refusing to be discouraged, we exited and sought the refuge of a weathered bench at the edge of the property, facing the bay. The crowded beach lay before us and the fashionable Inna Hotel lay behind us, but no one was rushing for our bench. In fact, everything seemed to fade as I suddenly realized we were sitting where I had sat fifty years ago.

As we sat there quietly holding hands, my mind recalled a myriad of treasured memories starting with Peace Corps training, meeting President Kennedy, teaching and coaching in Palembang, getting sick, and the assassination of President Kennedy. That was then, the 1960s. I then returned to the United States, met the woman who smiled from her heart, taught and studied throughout the world, enjoyed three marvelous children, and kept my promise made to God in that emergency situation in Palembang's Stanvac Oil hospital.

At some point that afternoon, I took a deep, refreshing breath and was finally able to say farewell to the old Kuta Beach Hotel and all that it signified for me. I had gratefully looked back on treasured memories, including those remaining months in 1964 when I returned to Palembang rejuvinated and well.

20

Lies

JAVANESE -

Just who was this Lies (pronounced "Lees"), whose beautifully-penned name drew my attention to the envelope? After the extended recuperation in exotic Bali, I returned to Palembang excited about teaching again. I went to my desk, eager to prepare a syllabus for my English literature class for the next semester. There on my desk lay a letter from a certain Lies, whose return address was Semarang, a city in East Java. But who was Lies? I couldn't remember meeting her, nor had I ever been to Semarang, except when I had traveled through by third-class train on my way to Bali. What was this communication?

As I read the letter, Lies explained that she had recently returned from Madison, Wisconsin, where she had lived for one year as a foreign exchange student. She said, "I loved every aspect of living in America—the school, the holidays and traditions, the food, the football games, my friends, and my American family. When I returned home to Indonesia, I left behind many friends and memories in Madison, and I now want to connect with Americans living in Indonesia."

So when she had recently been at a large wedding party in Semarang and met two Peace Corps volunteers, she was thrilled. On the seventh day of a Muslim wedding celebration, everyone in the vicinity is invited, so that included the two local Peace Corps coaches who were friends of mine and had traveled with me to Indonesia.

Excited to meet these Americans and to use her English, Lies happily connected with Bob and Ken. She explained that she was currently a freshman at the University of Semarang, majoring in English. Since she was on semester break, however, she would soon be traveling to Palembang with her father, the captain of a large oil tanker. This father and daughter were finally together on an adventure after her year of studying in America. One can assume that Pak, her father, would make sure that his daughter's trip to Palembang was memorable. After all, she was the captain's daughter, the apple of his eye.

In fact, it seemed probable that she was his princess on his ship, and she could ask for anything. Her picture, enclosed in the letter to me, revealed a beautiful Indonesian young lady. Being a ship captain's daughter, she was probably well aware of Indonesian courtesies and customs. She, however, had experienced a year living in the United States. Hence, she was bold enough to ask Bob and Ken if they, by chance, knew any Peace Corps volunteers in Palembang. Of course, they responded by giving her my name and address. And, yes, her father had given his approval for her to meet me—under his specified conditions.

Lies ended the letter by asking, "Paul, would you be interested in meeting my father and me when we come to Palembang?" Of course, I immediately responded, asking her to name the time and the place.

Her next letter explained that she would be traveling with her father on his oil tanker from Semarang to Palembang, a distance of approximately 415 miles. They would arrive the next Friday before 11:00 a.m. at Pier 3. She closed the note with, "Looking forward to meeting you."

Finally, that Friday dawned with a beautiful morning in Palembang. Anticipating Lies' arrival, I got to the dock early. After some searching, I found a bench at the end of a grassy park overlooking the harbor that would allow me to see Lies' ship dock.

Suddenly, questions began to swirl in my mind. "How will all this play out under the supervision of her father? Will this be an awkward meeting? (It certainly would be in the United States.) I wonder if it will be easy to talk with her. Do we really know enough of each other's language to say more than a few polite phrases? Oh, no! I have gotten myself into a mess!" As the appointed hour drew near, I began to doubt this whole adventure. "Do I really understand the strict cultural rules of meeting and interacting with an Indonesian young lady? What will her father think of me, especially if I embarrass or insult them unknowingly? I have seen her picture, but what is she really like?"

The ship docked at Pier 3. I could not see, however, any young lady waving or searching for a young American. The gangplank was lowered, yet no one rushed ashore. I continued to wait. When the first people appeared at the top of the ramp, I knew the time had come. I would focus carefully on the exiting passengers and somehow find the captain and Lies. The first people to disembark were a couple. As they got closer, I then recognized a distinguished gentleman dressed in blue maritime uniform escorting a graceful young lady wearing a tan skirt and a flowing white blouse that was partially covered by her black, braided hair cascading over her shoulder. Without any doubt, I stepped forward to meet Lies. Struck with her beauty, I attempted to present a collected, casual appearance as I walked anxiously toward them, first shaking the Captain's hand and then greeting his lovely daughter.

Since they had been traveling for several days, the captain suggested that they "get their land legs" by walking the path around the park. So off we went, with the captain on one side of his daughter and me on the other. Right away, the conversation flowed naturally. Perhaps the captain's experience of sailing the world had put him at ease in meeting all kinds of people, even a nervous young American. We skipped from topic to topic, discussing ship travel, the upcoming Olympic Games, Lies' year in Wisconsin, and even the political unrest in East Java. Whether speaking in English or Indonesian, the conversation flowed. The captain spoke English better than I spoke Indonesian, but we three shifted from one language to the other, caught up in our pleasure at being together. My respect for him and his joy at seeing his daughter happy seemed to cement our time together. Occasionally, I noticed him glancing furtively in my direction, as if to size me up. Honestly, I didn't blame him. Lies was his only daughter. This father, like fathers around the world, had a special commission to give her dignity through his love and wise protection.

As the conversation continued, the captain directed his attention to me, asking, "Paul, what kind of work did you do in the United States?"

"I taught English and coached American football and track at the secondary level," I answered.

"Ya! Ya! My daughter wants to teach English when she finishes at the university," he told me, with an accent that sounded Dutch.

My response of *"Baik! Baik!"* (Good! Good!) brought a broad smile to his face. I could tell that he was proud of Lies.

When I asked them about Lies' foreign exchange experience in Wisconsin, they both agreed that it had been a growing experience. The captain affirmed that absence had made his heart grow fonder for his daughter. Lies interjected, "Right on, Dad! That is why we are traveling together now. The year living overseas has also opened my eyes to the world before me. My interest in language has blossomed, especially because I lived with an American family. What a family!"

The captain chuckled, "Yes, she picked up American slang while she was there, and more!"

With a knowing smile, I added, "Living in a small two-bedroom house with an Indonesian family of six children and one bathroom has certainly made me comfortable with the culture and the language, too. The Peace Corps knows what it is doing by linking us with host families."

He responded saying, "Ya! Ya!" again, revealing possible Dutch language connections. Because Indonesia had been a Dutch colony until 1948, most of the educated Indonesians still spoke some Dutch in the 1960s.

Changing the subject, I asked the captain what it was like to be in charge of such a large, modern tanker. He smiled, explaining that he had spent twenty years in the maritime service, both under the Dutch and the Indonesians. These adventuresome years had allowed him, as a young man, to see the world and to sail "the seven seas." His main regret, however, was that he hadn't always been home for his family. As he glanced thoughtfully at Lies, she bowed her head out of respect for his confession.

Since it was going on one o'clock, I invited them to have lunch with me at a nearby restaurant overlooking the Musi River. As a Peace Corps volunteer, I normally would not have had enough money to treat guests to lunch. At the time, I still was paid thirty thousand rupiahs a month, equivalent to three dollars in American money. I paid twenty thousand rupiahs (two dollars) for room and board, and that left ten thousand rupiahs (one dollar) to live on and to run my motorbike. Of course, no Indonesian could fathom that I lived on such a salary because they believed all Americans were wealthy. So whenever I ran out of money for petrol midway through the month, I had to tell my friends that my motorbike was broken, an excuse they could accept. Otherwise, they would have thought I was lying if I had said I had no money. However, I had recently received a Christmas card from my family with ten dollars enclosed. And, therefore, my story of treating the captain and Lies to lunch can honestly continue.

When we got to the Ancol Restaurant, a trade wind coming off the Musi River provided refreshing relief from the tropical humidity. We found a small, remote table for three close to the water's edge. The captain laughed as he said in a joking tone, "Paul, I hope this is not one of those restaurants that serves the delicacy of 'Palembang dog.'" I assured him it wasn't, but we did have a lunch of Palembang's popular cuisine: fried rice, fried pineapple, and Sumatran tea. To add to the atmosphere, soft Indonesian music mingled with the breezes of the afternoon trade wind.

So far, this visit had been a threesome, but that was the custom for meeting a young woman in Indonesia. Lies and I did have the opportunity to meet, but we both were subject to her father's oversight. Nevertheless, everything about our first visit was enchanting, except that the time flew by so quickly. Luck was with us, however, for the captain announced that he had to return to the ship to prepare for their departure the following morning. Before he excused himself, I thanked him for bringing Lies to Palembang. He smiled at me and said encouragingly, "I hope to see you again, Paul," Then turning to Lies, he reminded, "Dinner will be at six." So that was how the chaperone system was working in Indonesia, even among the sophisticated class who boasted contact with the wider world.

In any case, Lies and I were finally together, sitting on the same bench where I first saw her father's ship dock. She whispered, "Whew! I didn't know if Papa would ever excuse himself for dinner, where he always hosts the evening meal." By then, I was impressed with Lies' fun spirit and maturity. Her quiet, reassuring voice spoke peace and serenity to my tired soul. Why so tired? I had weathered the previous months of amoebic dysentery, near death, the miraculous rescue, and the desperation of homesickness. Recuperating on a tropical beach had been almost perfect, but I had a growing sense that I wanted to share my life experiences with someone else. Granted, I had spent many hours and days watching the sunrises and sunsets alone, but perhaps it gave me the needed opportunity to question the purpose of my life, my reasons to stay in Indonesia, and just what my future might hold. Yet, I felt alone. Why so tired? I was physically and emotionally spent. So this meeting at Pier 3 did bring peace to my tired soul, and it brought a beautiful girl into my life. I felt alive again.

In fact, I was smitten when I looked into Lies' sparkling eyes, joined her in spontaneous laughter, and enjoyed relaxed conversation. It was a lighthearted, happy time; the more serious talks were to follow. This seemed such a genuine time together. I must admit that the time was like a life preserver to a weakened, drowning man. The more we talked, the more I got lost in her smile. I understood more clearly that day the Balinese belief that some young women smile only from their eyes, but others smile from deep within their hearts. This confident and beautiful lady was for real.

We said our reluctant goodbyes, having quietly enjoyed each other's company, according to her customs. I knew from Peace Corps training that young couples in Indonesian culture were not permitted to be alone without a chaperone. And even then, physical contact of any kind, such as innocently holding hands, was not allowed in public places. Public display of affection was certainly taboo and in poor taste. In no way was I going to cheapen Lies' reputation or dishonor her father by holding her hand, as much as I wanted to. I watched her ascend the gangplank to the ship's open hatch. At the top of the ramp, she stopped momentarily and waved goodbye.

Immediately I went home, pushed aside the English literature syllabus I had been working on, and started a letter to Lies. This letter was the first of many between Lies and me. Her letters were always filled with encouragement and packed with memorable stories of her freshman year at Semarang University. She continued to reminisce about her experiences of living in the United States, and she was proud of her fluency in English. She openly talked positively about American culture and the people, a refreshing viewpoint when all around me the media spewed distain for America and the West. Even she recognized the public bias that was a reality for that period of time.

In my letters, I shared about life in Palembang, my enjoyable classes, friends, and the excitement over progress in the sports programs. When I complained about difficulties, especially in the area of sports, Lies often replied, "Slowly, slowly, Paul. At least you are providing an opportunity for my people to perform better, and I know your students enjoy you. Didn't you say in your last letter that the discus and shot-put competitors were performing better after participating in the weight training programs? And didn't your girls' volleyball team win their last competition? Remember, go slowly, Paul."

The post office became a regular stop on my way home from teaching at the university or from coaching. Even when the coaching clinic was out in a remote area, I would make sure my detour always included a stop at the local post office. There might be the letters from home and friends, but, of course, I was really looking for letters from Semarang and that special young lady.

The Indonesia of the 1960s was a far cry from today's budding commercial center in Southeast Asia. Few Westerners, especially Americans, knew of this country. In fact, the current fads of vacationing in touristy Kuta Beach, surfing in Lombok, and scuba diving in the Gili Islands were unknown to Americans then. In many cases, especially in the more remote villages, Westerners were seldom seen. As a result, I was often an anomaly, sometimes of great interest, even at a place as simple as the post office.

I walked into the post office wearing a t-shirt and shorts after an afternoon of coaching. Yet again, I ignored stares, waited in line, and hoped for word from Lies. Suddenly, to my surprise, I felt a pinch of pain on my arm as if bitten by an insect. Looking down, I spotted someone curiously pulling at the dark hair on my arm. *"Lucu! Lucu!"* (Funny! Funny!), chortled the man who had discovered that Westerners have hair on their arms and legs, unlike Indonesians. This was not the first time I was the object of such curiosity. In fact, as I exited the post office that same day and stopped to read the letter from Lies, I was momentarily unaware of a group of people peering over both of my shoulders. I was then shocked unexpectedly out of my fog when one of the gawkers, pointing to the wording in my letter, actually asked in Indonesian, "What does that word mean?" Nothing, not even pesky intruders, could distract me from the good news in the letter.

Lies would be on her father's ship, which was making an oil run to Palembang the following month. Of course, I wrote her back immediately, promising to meet her at the same park bench near Pier 3.

And that is where I was a month later when her father's ship arrived. Time went slowly until the gangplank was lowered. At the top of the ramp stood two dignified people, this time smiling at me. I noticed that they talked softly as they strolled down the gangplank. There was no denying their love for one another. I thought to myself, "I hope that this is the type of relationship I will have with my daughters someday."

Once again, we three sat on the same old park bench talking about our worlds; Lies and I chitchatted about our university lives, she as a student and I as a professor. She giggled when I quoted a few lines in Middle English from *Canterbury Tales*. "That's not English. You are just trying to fool me." Teasing, she added, "I could be your student if I were studying at the University of Sriwidjaja."

"Yes, Lies, you would get to be with some of the finest students I have ever taught," I responded. "They even ask if they can come for extra tutorials on Saturday mornings. With your bright mind and sparkling personality, you would fit in perfectly. Believe me, my students are studying hard, and we are enjoying the results. We have lively discussions and rewarding times analyzing English literature. There is a fun Scottish ballad, 'Get Up and Bar the Door,' which my students acted out last week. It's a dialogue between a husband and wife arguing about who will get up and secure the door during a freezing, stormy night. You know. You lived in Madison, Wisconsin, in the winter! Well, when I asked the students who won the argument, they chuckled and agreed that the wife came out the victor." Proudly, I added, "My students even memorized the first eighteen lines of the prologue to *Canterbury Tales*."

Lies and I also talked about topics that were sometimes too politically sensitive to discuss in letters. There had been protests in Lies' hometown of Semarang against the United States. Even closer to Lies' university world, demonstrators had forced the closure of the USIS library that students used for research and study. This was a dangerous time in Indonesia as the communists were vying for control.

Being the captain of a large oil tanker, it was not prudent for Lies' father to engage in such talk, so before long, the captain changed the subject by saying, "Paul, it is my turn to treat you. I know an excellent fish restaurant near the water. Let's give it a try." Remembering that the Peace Corps had cautioned about discussing politics or religion, I jumped at the opportunity to talk about lighter topics and enjoy lunch with Lies.

After a lunch of fish and chips, we walked back to our bench. And again, the captain made an excuse that he had to return to his ship immediately, claiming that he had important duties aboard ship in preparation for departure the next day. As he went up the gangplank, he smiled at us both and then said to Lies, "Remember, dinner at six o'clock." Realizing that I might not see him again this trip, I walked over to the gangplank and said my goodbyes to him with a firm, sincere handshake. He smiled at me, saying, "Remember, Paul, Lies is my most prized possession, God's gift to me."

"Yes, sir, I understand and respect that," I responded.

As I returned to the bench, I sat down next to Lies, closer than we had been before. As the trade winds blew cooler temperatures, I enjoyed her warmth next to me and the velvet touch of her hand on mine, hidden from public view. The touch was discreet and, of course, magical for me. I looked into her radiant, almond-shaped eyes with the hope that I was not dreaming. Again, we talked. It seemed like beautiful lines of poetry that defied words but not the human heart. I realized I was falling hard for Lies. How could this be? We had only known each other for a couple of months and written many letters to each other, but we had only seen each other twice. She had come into my life at the right time. Her sparkling personality and quiet voice had brought healing to my weakened body and spirit. Nevertheless, with time being the enemy of love, I walked Lies to the gangplank and, with a myriad of emotions, watched her gracefully begin to ascend the ramp. Then she slowly and deliberately turned toward me and said a soft, reluctant goodbye.

I again said, "I will write you soon."

Smiling from her heart and fighting back tears, she responded, "Soon, please soon, Paul."

That night, I anguished over our parting. We did continue to write for many months. But during that time, we came to realize that we each had deep commitments to our different cultures, our different faiths, and our love for "homeland." At some point, I knew that I could not selfishly take Lies away from all she loved, that my love had to embrace more than merely "wanting." True, our relationship had been brief. Nevertheless, it had been wholesome and winsomely innocent, forging deep within me a life priority to find the woman whom I would eventually marry, a woman who would smile from deep within her heart.

21

Selamat Tinggal

As I was getting out of the bemo at the Palembang airport, one of my students from my morning ELS class rode up to the curb on his black bike, yelling, "Good morning, Mr. Paul." Yes, this was the Omar who had run me over on Sudirman Boulevard soon after I began teaching at the university. And, yes, Omar's English was correct this time. He should have gotten it right after being in my classes for two years! It was a "good" morning. Omar and friends were at the airport to see me off and, in a real sense, we all were celebrating our success at having studied and interacted and tasted life together for two years. For everyone involved, we had certainly grown and changed, especially this West Coast guy, who was now heading back home to California—forever changed.

Earlier that day, as the bemo had lugged down the heavily trafficked Sudirman Boulevard heading to Palembang Airport, I tried to remember Palembang on that humid afternoon when I first arrived there two years previously. This time, however, I did not recoil from the dirty streets, the open sewers, and the pungent smells, but rather I focused on the wonderful images of the people whom I had grown to love and respect through our varied experiences together.

I took from my shirt pocket the last letter Lies had sent to me. She expressed her regret that we didn't have enough time together. Lies, however, did share her love and hope that we would continue to write. She apologized for the latest demonstrations against the United States and thanked me for my service to her country and for being a good representative of my country. I found myself wishing that she were seated next to me so that I could tell her how thankful I was that she had been a beautiful part of my life. I put her wrinkled letter back into my shirt pocket as the bemo drove up to the airport drop-off curb.

Carrying my battered suitcase, which had been my "sidekick" through many adventures, I walked into the waiting room, surprised to see a host of friends, students, university officials, and KOGOR officials waiting to say *selamat jalan* (goodbye, have a safe journey) to me. It was just like my Indonesian friends to surprise me like this. They had done it once before when I was sick in the hospital, and again, they were there, revealing their faithfulness. Many, through their caring actions, had helped to strengthen my faith and my resolve to "stay the course." And I trust that they benefitted from my relationships with them.

As I slowly looked around at each person standing in the room to thank them, images of the two years flashed before me.

There stood several people from the university. Some students held signs that said "Goodbye, Mr. Paul. Please come again." Other students carried small tokens of their appreciation. By that time, Omar, having tied that black bike to a tree outside the departure waiting area, had joined the student group. Today, just the memory of Omar and his "good morning/ evening" greeting brings a smile to my spirit and remains as a lasting gift in my mind.

Next to those students stood Dr. Hardjono (the rektor of Sriwidjaja University) and her driver. They had come to the airport in the same truck that had regularly transported other instructors and me to the university each day. Dr. Hardjono's solid support and encouragement never swayed. She taught me the meaning of courage through her professional administration of a prominent university during times of turmoil. She fought for high standards and never once caved in to rival pressures.

Standing in another group, with a smile on his face, was Major Askar, a leader in KOGOR who believed in sports for the people. Major Askar led the uphill battle for multi-pronged sport programs, not only for his children but for all the young people of Palembang. There were no Olympic competitors there to say goodbye, but Palembang could claim some bright athletic stars on the horizon, and interest in sports had grown.

Standing next to Major Askar, also with beaming faces, were Pak and Ibu Bahar. Pak worked for Major Askar as a sports official. I remembered the day when Pak showed up at the Hotel Swarma Dwipa to check up on us during our first month in Palembang. He was so disturbed at our living conditions there that he offered us accommodations in his own small home. Pak had put his whole family in jeopardy because of his decision.

What fine, courageous people! I could genuinely refer to them with the respectful terms *Pak* and *Ibu*.

Missing from that collage of people who came to say goodbye were two men who had greatly influenced my stay in Palembang. Mr. Benteng, who had reached into the depth of his anger by attempting to threaten and drive me out of the university, had not accomplished his goal. Although Mr. Benteng was not at Palembang Airport with the Indonesians wishing me a safe journey home *(selamat jalan)*, I am certain he was present and active the following year when the communists launched their bloody coup to overtake Indonesia. He failed again.

Also missing that day was Bob Gonia. He had reached out to me in spite of his own grief, helped me grow as a man, and urged me to reach deep within myself by recognizing that it is not "all about me." Bob, you started me on a lifelong journey to be the person God has designed me to be. Thank you, Bob, for sounding the starting gun. I'm still running.

Taking one last look at my friends gathered in that departure lounge, I said, *"Selamat tinggal,"* (goodbye) and headed toward the plane and toward a new path on my life journey.

Epilogue

Over the years, people who marveled or laughed or cried at the accounts of my years with the Peace Corps in Indonesia have suggested that I capture the adventures in a memoir.

In fact, the idea first came many years ago from students who quipped, "Mr. B., you just have to write that story in a book." The time I have spent researching, confirming, and detailing those years has convinced me, once more, that young people need to be encouraged to reach out courageously and to give themselves opportunities that lie beyond their comfort zones.

I have cheered on those who have looked to the Peace Corps or to other personal challenges. My advice, "Do it!", has always been with an awareness that there may be unseen hardships—and unexpected blessings. I certainly have identified with young people in school or post-schooling who are forging their unique paths.

I have, however, become keenly aware that I am definitely in the baby-boomer generation. I did not want to admit it until one simple conversation I had with my wife. After retiring from forty-two years of teaching and still enjoying interacting with young people, I could not just hang up my teaching hat. I taught six more years at two schools that asked me to "keep on" doing what I loved. At the end of each teaching commitment, I quipped, "I'm retiring again." Finally, my wife pointed out that I had retired three times. In fact, she asked when I planned to retire for good. Then there came an opportunity to volunteer to teach in Indonesia for a short stint. We packed our bags and "did it." "Hey!" we both chuckled. "Let's always try to be 'retired for *good.*'"

A Franciscan Benediction

May God bless you with a restless discomfort
About easy answers, half-truths, and superficial relationships,
So that you may seek truth boldly and love deep within your heart.

May God bless you with holy anger at injustice, oppression,
And exploitation of people, so that you may tirelessly work for
justice, freedom, and peace among all people.

May God bless you with enough foolishness to believe that
You really can make a difference in this world, so that you are able,
With God's grace, to do what others claim cannot be done.

And the blessing of God, the Supreme Majesty and our Creator,
Jesus Christ the Incarnate Word who is our Brother and Savior,
and the Holy Spirit, our Advocate and Guide, be with you
and remain with you, this day and forevermore. Amen.

Glossary of Indonesian Terms

Apa kabar – How are you?

Baik – fine; good

Berhenti – stop

Berani – brave; courageous

Hilang – lost

Hari – day

Hari natal – Merry Christmas

Hati, hati – careful

Ibu – term of respect for mother; elder

Kampung – poor, small village, or section of a larger city

Lucu – funny

Maaf – I beg your pardon; sorry

Makan – eat

Makan pagi – breakfast

Makan siang – lunch

Makan malam – dinner

Mandi – bath

Rumah makan – restaurant

Pak – term of respect for father; elder

Selamat pagi – good morning

Selamat siang – good afternoon

Selamat malam – good evening

Selamat tinggal – goodbye

Selamat tidur – good night

Terima kashi – thank you

Tidak – no

Tidak baik – not good

Further Readings on Indonesia

Donovan, Robert J. *P.T. 109: John F. Kennedy in WWII*. New York: McGraw-Hill, 2001.

Kennedy, John F. *Profiles in Courage*. New York: Harper Collins Learning Prebound, 2006.

Koch, Christopher, J. *The Year of Living Dangerously*. New York: Penguin Books, 1983.

Ricklefs, M.C. *A History of Modern Indonesia Since c.1200*. Third Ed. Stanford: Stanford
University Press, 2001.

Rose, Darlene Deibler. *Evidence Not Seen*. San Francisco: Harper San Francisco, 1990.

Vickers, Adrian. *A History of Modern Indonesia*. Cambridge: Cambridge University Press, 2005.

Williams, Maslyn: *Five Journeys from Jakarta*. New York: William Morrow and Company, 1965.

Winchester, Simon. *The Day the World Exploded: August 27, 1883*. New York: Harper Collins
Publishers, 2003.

Winston, Arlita Morken. *Heart-Cry*. Victoria, Canada: Trafford Publishing, 2007.

About the Author

Paul Burghdorf continues to make Southern California his home base. He recently concluded fifty years of teaching and coaching. He remains grateful to the Glendale Unified School District, which allowed him (and his family) leave opportunities to teach overseas. Each time, he returned eager to share more of his life stories and to encourage students to dream big. Paul continues to enjoy working out, exploring the High Sierras, and looking for ways he can participate in "the classroom"— the best place in the world.

CPSIA information can be obtained at www.ICGtesting.com
Printed in the USA
BVOW011642270213

314321BV00001B/138/P